ANATOLIY DRAHAN

the Great Book of Ukraine

*Interesting Stories, Ukrainian History & Random Facts
About Ukraine (History & Fun Facts)*

First edition

This book was professionally typeset on Reedsy.
Find out more at reedsy.com

Contents

Introduction

What do you know about Ukraine, the amazing country in the east of Europe that impresses with its history, distinctive culture, and exciting traditions? Did you know that the author of the Christmas carol 'Carol of Bells' is Ukrainian Mykola Lysenko?

Do you know why they call Ukrainian cutlets 'Chicken Kyiv'?

Did you know that Ukrainian Yuriy Budyak saved the life of future British Prime Minister Winston Churchill?

What about the fact that Zaporizhian Sich was the first democracy in Europe, where Hetman was elected by the general assembly long before European parliamentarians appeared?

If not, then this book is for you. You can learn many new facts about Ukraine and its brave people.

The book is aimed at a broad audience, with a few questions at the end of each chapter to help you learn more about Ukraine.

Ukrainian Symbols

How Ukraine Got Its Name

The name "Ukraine" is quite ancient. The first written mention dates back to 1187. The Ipatievskaya Chronicle mentions the death of Prince Vladimir Glebovich of Pereyaslavl, for whom "all Ukraine wept. In the Galitsko-Volynsky Chronicle of 1213, "Ukrainians" and "Ukraine" are used. Interestingly, the same lands were called Ukraine or

Rus in the ancient texts. Why were both names used?

In ancient times on the territory of modern Ukraine, there was a state of Rus with its capital in Kyiv. In the 9th century, Rus was relatively small and covered the modern Kiev, Chernihiv, Zhytomyr, and Cherkasy regions. But the campaigns of princes Sviatoslav, Vladimir the Great, and Yaroslav the Wise expanded the lands of Kievan Rus from the Baltic Sea in the north to the Black Sea in the south, from Belarus in the west to the Kuban in the east.

At the same time, the chroniclers came up with an exciting form to distinguish Rus's old and newly annexed territories. That's why the historic center around Kyiv was called "the country. Herein lies the clue of the name of our state: it comes from the word "country (krayina- ukr)," and the preposition "at"(u -ukr) is used to denote something inside. Thus, "Ukraine" means "territory within the country" or "the central part of the state - the lands of modern Ukraine occupied the central region on the map of Kievan Rus. And the remote outskirts, lost in the thickets and swamps, were just the territory of the future Moscow principality.

The name "Ukraine" became more popular in the times of the Cossacks and the Polish-Lithuanian Commonwealth. It is found in documents, letters, and writings of clergy members. That was the name given to the territory of the Dnieper region, located along the Dnieper River. Later, it began to spread to other areas, especially on the left bank.

It is believed that the change from Rus to Ukraine was necessary and was a protest against the tsarist policy of Russia, which was intended to turn the Ukrainian nation into the Russian nation. This is rumored why the Moscow Empire appropriated the name "Rus" for itself, turning it into Russia over time. This was to contribute to the loss of our identity. And when it became clear that Ukrainians continue to try to be independent and cannot eradicate this name. It was decided to discredit it. Therefore, Ukraine began to be treated as "the outskirts of Russia.

The name "Ukraine" went a long way to official recognition in 1991 when it proclaimed its independence. Although the origin of the term is ancient, many Russian imperialists still cannot accept it, relying on the fact that they did not want to recognize it for a long time officially.

Why is the Ukrainian Flag Yellow and Blue?

The combination of blue and yellow is one of the oldest modern national flags of all continents. It was used in Kyiv as early as before Christianity. But what do these colors mean?

Blue has long symbolized a clear and peaceful sky, while yellow, a symbol of labor and prosperity, was the color of a grain field. But there are other definitions, too. Yellow and blue combine the main symbols of life - the golden sun in blue space. Yellow and blue are also fire and water, masculine and feminine.

Ukrainian Cossacks also used this combination of colors. Since the XVIII century, the flags of the Zaporozhian Army were increasingly made on blue cloth, where yellow paint was used to draw stars, crosses, weapons, or figures of saints. These two colors were often used in everyday life, in Cossack clothes, and even by the church.

The history of the Ukrainian flag is thorny and complicated. Prolonged wars, loss of autonomy, and joining large empires have forced for some time to put aside thoughts about the state flag. In recent times meaningless disputes among supporters of the collapse of Ukrainian statehood about the incorrect placement of colors on the flag still cause tension in society.

They could not even invent anything about the Ukrainian flag: that it was 'turned over' by hetman Pavlo Skoropadskiy, that 'traitor' Ivan Mazepa received it from Swedes, and that the location of colors does not correspond to rules of heraldry (the science of flags), and even that according to feng shui, place of blue over yellow means that supposedly water fills the fire and that symbolizes recession.

To dispel myths about the state flag of Ukraine, let's learn more about the history of the Ukrainian state flag.

The ancient Ukrainian flags had a triangular wedge shape. Thus, in the times of Kievan Rus, the red flag with a trident tongue was the most widespread. And later, in the XIV century, blue and yellow began to appear on Ukrainian flags: for example, in 1848, they were represented on the flag of the Galicia-Volyn principality and also on coats of arms of medieval cities, nobles, and princes. From the 18th century onwards, a blue cloth was increasingly used as a background for the flag of the Zaporizhian Knights. They were shown wearing golden trousers with golden ornaments and armatures.

From 1917 to 1921, during the Ukrainian Revolution, the blue and yellow cloth was the national flag of the Ukrainian People's Republic and the Ukrainian State, headed by Pavlo Skoropadsky.

In the Dnieper region, the colors of the Ukrainian flag are as follows: blue symbolizes the sky, and yellow the ripe wheat field.

Analyzing the historical events, we can confidently say that the blue-yellow flag of the twentieth century was a symbol of Ukrainian national resistance against the Communist-Russian occupation.

And when the USSR collapsed, the Ukrainian two-color flag began to be used as the state flag of independent Ukraine.

Origin of the Ukrainian Coat of Arms - Trident

The Trident is an essential emblem of Ukraine. It is a central element of small and large Ukrainian coats of arms.

It should be noted that at the moment, Ukraine officially approved only a small coat of arms; the big one exists only in the form of several projects.

The Small Coat of Arms of Ukraine is a blue shield with a golden (yellow) border, which shows a golden (yellow) trident. As the state symbol, it was adopted by the Verkhovna Rada on February 19, 1992.

The most exciting part of the Ukrainian coat of arms is the Trident in terms of heraldry. This is an ancient symbol whose history starts long before the blond Vikings founded the city on the Dnieper river cliffs - the future capital of independent Ukraine.

When people talk about Ukrainian trident, they usually mention Vladimir the Great and other Old Russian princes and discuss the Norman origin of the symbol. It was brought to the banks of the Dnieper by fierce Scandinavian warriors. The history of the trident is much more prosperous, and the Normans were not the first to like the symbol. The trident was a ubiquitous sign, the image of which was revered by many different people.

Since antiquity, it has been used, with the trident most often favored by people whose lives were linked to the sea. After all, among other things, it is also an instrument of fishing. Not without reason, the trident is the main attribute of Poseidon - the god of seas and oceans in Greek mythology.

The trident was armed by Inanna - the main female deity in the Sumerian pantheon of gods. Sumerians believed that once it was Inanna who ruled a fairy-tale country, Aratta - an analog of the Russian Belovodyas or Tibetan Shambhala. In Mesopotamia, there was another god with a trident - Ishkur. He was subject to thunder, lightning, and various atmospheric precipitations. The trident was also the symbol of Marduk, the supreme deity of ancient Babylon.

The images of the trident are found in the temples of the Minoan civilization; it was one of the attributes of the Hittite gods and is widely represented in the Vedic tradition. In Hinduism, several deities used a trident. He was the constant attribute of the god Varuna, who was considered the patron saint of waters and Shiva and his warrior consort Durga. The god of fire, Agni, is often depicted with a trident.

The Trident can also be considered one of the main symbols of Buddhism: in this major world religion. It represents the three jewels of Buddha.

The Trident was a symbol of supreme power in the Genghisid Empire and is still revered in Mongolia. For many centuries, the trident-tamga was the symbol of the Girey family - the rulers of the Crimean Khanate.

In medieval Europe, the Trident was most popular in Scandinavia. It was worshiped as a sign of supreme power, a military symbol, and used on coins. In addition to the Trident, there are also depictions of the two-tongue. We can add that the image trident became more and more stylized in the early Middle Ages.

The Vikings brought the trident to the land of Russia. He was the sign of the Rurikovich family - founders of the ancient Russian state. The basic version says that the trident was the stylized image of the sacred falcon Rarog - a bird presented in Scandinavian and Slavic mythology.

There is another hypothesis. It is connected with another sacred bird of the Normans - the raven of the god Odin. His image can often be found on Scandinavian jewelry, coins, banners, amulets, etc.

One thing is clear: initially, a trident was just a generic coat of arms of Rurikids, their military emblem, and only at the time did it turn into a national logo. During the heyday of Kievan Rus, this symbol was put on coins, stamps and ceramics and used in murals. For instance, on the coins of Prince Vladimir Svyatoslavovich, there was a depiction of the ruler on one side and the coat of arms of a trident on the other.

The history of Ukraine is rich and varied. After the disintegration of the ancient Kyiv state, a number of appanage principalities were formed within its borders, each of which used its symbols. It should be noted that during the Lithuanian and Polish periods, the Trident was not used in the coats of arms of Ukrainian lands.

In 1917 it was proclaimed the establishment of an independent Ukrainian state and immediately raised the question of its official symbols. A special commission was formed to deal with this problem. As an emblem of the UNR, various historic symbols were considered: Zaporizhzhia Cossack with a musket, Archistratigus Michael, and others.

Historian and one of the leaders of the Central Rada, Mykhailo Hrushevsky, suggested using a princely trident of Kievan Rus as a small coat of arms. At the beginning of 1918, it was officially approved as an emblem of the Ukrainian People's Republic. Even earlier, Trident appeared on the first Ukrainian banknotes.

The Trident was also used as a coat of arms in Ukraine during the rule of Hetman Skoropadskyi and under the Directory. At the same time, the first sketches of an oversized state coat of arms, based on the same Trident, appeared.

During the Soviet period, Trident continued to be used as a symbol of the national liberation movement to create a Ukrainian national state. It was widely represented in badges and insignia and the decoration system of the Ukrainian Insurgent Army.

As it was already mentioned above, the Trident as the official coat of arms of Ukraine was approved on February 19, 1992.

Fun facts about Ukraine

Interesting Facts About Zaporizhzhia Cossacks

Probably no one will argue that the Cossacks are quite an interesting "phenomenon" in Ukrainian and world history. However, along with their courage, strength, cunning, and intelligence, a bit of mysticism often makes them something more than just warriors. So, maybe the Cossacks were not so ordinary indeed?

Here are some interesting facts about Ukrainian knights:

Apart from weapons, strength, and the ability to fight well, the Cossacks had another significant advantage: their wit and cunning. They usually managed to sneak up on their enemies unnoticed and take them by surprise. Of course, this added to their chances of victory.

One can also think of the original boat, which the Cossacks used for military campaigns. It can be called the "ancestor" of modern submarines, as strange as it may sound. It consisted of two bottoms, between which a weight was placed to submerge the vessel in the water. In this way, the Cossacks sailed stealthily up to their enemies. Before the attack, the cargo would be thrown out, and the vessel would suddenly rise to the surface. Of course, this was a surprise for the enemy because no one expected that the Zaporozhian army could appear from the depths of the sea. For the same thing, they used upside-down "seagulls" - famous Cossack boats that were not afraid of storms or enemy warships. They were often turned upside down to sneak up on the enemy.

The Zaporizhian Sich is rightly called the first democratic union in the world. It is not surprising that many people came here because of social injustice. All the issues that concerned the life and activity of the Cossacks were resolved by voting at the councils.

During peacetime, it is believed that the leading entertainment of the Cossacks was drinking. But of course, there was also drinking. But the Cossacks also liked cultural entertainment: they played music, sang songs, danced, and held showdowns to amuse themselves and others. They also had much to do at home, as there were no women at the Sich, so they had to cope by themselves.

But during the campaigns, it was strictly forbidden to get drunk. Violation of this rule was tantamount to treason and could be punished with death.

The family life of a Cossack was difficult, if there was one at all. But they found their brethren at the Sich, for whom they were ready to give up everything. It is said that the Cossacks even had a special ritual during which the warriors would exchange their crosses. It was a symbol of their loyalty to each other.

The Sichi laws were stringent. If a Cossack would steal or kill a fellow soldier, he would not only pay with his life but would rather brutally do it: he would be buried alive with the deceased or beaten with clubs, which often ended fatally. So, yes, you could say that it was not humane, but the discipline was excellent.

There were Cossacks who were called "characterists". It was believed that they descended from the ancient pagan wise men, who had secret knowledge and could predict the future. Some historians hold the theory that after adopting Christianity in Rus, they were persecuted by the princes and Greeks. Therefore magi-pagans created small associations far away from big cities - Sichi. There they taught the future warriors martial arts, rituals, and customs. It was said about the priests that they "could not be killed by fire, water, swords, or usual bullets, except the silver one", and that they "could open locks without keys, float on boats on the floor like on the sea waves, cross the river on mats of vines, take red-hot cores in their bare hands, see for several versts around themselves, be at the bottom of the river, climb in and out of tightly knotted or even sewn bags, "turn" into cats, turn people into bushes, horsemen into birds, climb into an ordinary bucket and swim hundreds, thousands of meters underwater in it."

The Cossacks used their knowledge and borrowed fighting techniques from other nations. It is said that not only Ukrainians but also representatives of about 20 different nations: Russians, Poles, Moldavians, and Belarusians, lived at the Sich. In addition, the Cossacks and hetmans often traveled around the world and were introduced to the culture and customs of other countries.

It was independent, and all the European countries have tried to establish diplomatic relations with it.

The Cossacks didn't have one flag, but in the 17th century, it was the main flag of the Zaporizhian state. It had the Archangel Michael depicted on the red background on one side and a white cross, golden sun, crescent, and stars on the other. A Cossack with a musket was a particular coat of arms.

Interestingly, the six-pointed star was often depicted on Cossack banners. However, it did not concern the Jewish people in any way. Instead, it was a symbol of magic or an emblem of certain clans in ancient times. Back then, it was a rather famous sign that stood for harmony.

12

As for the distinctive hairstyle and mustache of Ukrainian knights, it is said that Cossacks inherited it from their pagan ancestors. The tradition of shaving your head and face was inherited from the local tribes to Kievan Rus and eventually reached the Cossacks. Historians say that the ancient Slavs had no gods with beards or long hair, so this image had been considered divine since ancient times. Another legend has it that the Cossacks considered themselves too sinful for Heaven. So, when they went to hell, God would have mercy on them and pull them out by the scruff of the neck. In general, such a legend was not only practised by Cossacks. In ancient times Egyptian pharaohs, Indians of some tribes, Tatars, Indians, Persians, and Japanese samurai also followed these pratices. The long forelock symbolized a "ray of sunshine" for many nations". The difference between the Cossacks was that they styled their long foreheads while the others left it in the middle of their heads or at the nape of their necks. And Cossacks used to say: if I am lost in the war, an angel will carry me to the sky because of my chub.

The Cossacks had an attractive custom. Their huts were always open. A traveler or a passer-by could enter them, wait, eat something to eat, and go on his journey. And this even if the owner was not at home. However, there was a strict rule. One should not take anything out of the hut; otherwise, there would be punishment. And when someone finds something in the Sich, they tie it to a high pole. If the owner is not found within three days, the thing will have the one who found it.

They say that on Khortitsa Island, a giant oak tree is still glorified in Cossack songs and legends. Some say that the Cossacks held their rituals under it when going to battle. The rumor is that the tree is already 700 years old.

There are also many theories regarding the origin of 'Cossack'. Some Polish scholars believe that the word originated from the notorious ringleader Kozak, who fought masterfully against the Tatars. It originated from the word goat because the Cossacks were very clever and could get their way anywhere. In Turkish, "Cossack" meant "vagabond, robber." Logically, the Turks gave the Cossacks that nickname. The nickname stuck in Ukraine and eventually lost its negative connotations.

It is said that Cossacks also made their way to America. It is said that John

Smith, one of the founders of the first British settlement on the American continent, had earlier taken part in the Catholic fight against the Tartars and the Turks. During one of the battles, he was taken prisoner, where he stayed until the Cossacks rescued him. Subsequently, he stayed at the Sich, and from there, he returned to England, where he invited the Cossacks. At this time, the British decided to establish the first colony in America. So it is said that John Smith set off on his journey, taking with him some Cossacks who had expressed a desire.

Interesting Facts About Ukraine

1. Ukraine is located in Eastern Europe; the European center is in Ukraine! There is a two-meter high sign, which certifies the geographical center of Europe, on the part of the twisting mountain road Rakhiv-Uzhgorod. In 1887 (at that time, the Zakarpattya region belonged to Austria-Hungary), to build a railway, engineers found out that somewhere in this area must be the center of Europe. Invited Viennese scientists confirmed the conjecture

and installed a geodesic sign in the form of a concrete slab, attesting to their finding.

2. The Ukrainian Philip Orlik is believed to have created one of the world's first constitutions. The document was created as an agreement between Hetman of Zaporozhian troops Pylyp Orlyk and Styshynas and Cossacks of the forces. It was called the "Constitution of Rights and Freedoms of Zaporozhian troops".

3. Taras Shevchenko is a prominent cultural figure with the most significant number of monuments. Ukrainian Kobzar has 1384 monuments all over the world. Taras Shevchenko, a Roman patrician, makes a speech in Rome; in Brazil, he is depicted as a young man with a book in his hands; in Poland, he is depicted as a young boy with a candle.

4. Scientists testify that the oldest settlement of Homo sapiens was found at the Mezhyretska Station in Ukraine. One of the oldest maps ever seen, a map has also been found there. The age of the map is 15 000 years.

5. The Kyiv Arsenalna metro station is the deepest in the world. Its depth is 105,5 meters. The station's design is the so-called English type - inside, the station has a short hall, i.e., the distance from the escalators to the wall is straightforward.

6. Have you heard of the route "from the Varangians to the Greeks"? It passed through Ukraine and was one of the most extensive trade waterways. It was 3,000 km long, connecting the north of Kievan Rus and Byzantium.

This route went from the Varangian (Baltic) Sea by the Gulf of Finland along the river Neva and the Lake Ladoga, then the river Volkhov, the Lake Ilmen, the river Lovattu, then dragged by boats to the Dnieper, then the Rusynian (Black) Sea along the western shore to Constantinople (now Istanbul). They also changed their route - along the Odra to Krakow to Galicia via Zvenigorod, Plisnesk, and Galich.

Legends and Myths about Ivan Sirko

Ivan Sirko's life is shrouded in legends; no one can tell which is factual or fiction.

They say that Ivan Sirko, ataman of Zaporizhzhia Cossacks:

- He did not lose a single battle;

- He signed the famous letter of the Cossacks to the Turkish Sultan;

- He participated in the capture of the fortress of Dunkirk during the Thirty Years' War;

- After his death, the Cossacks defeated their enemies by throwing his severed arm forward;

- In 1812, Ivan Sirko's arm was carried three times around Moscow occupied by the French, and the fate of the war was sealed;

- He was called a werewolf and a character, and the Turks called him Urus-Shaitan.

What is true, and what is a myth? And who was Ivan Sirko?

The y

ear and place of birth of Ivan Sirko are unknown. According to some sources, he was born in Podolia's nobleman family. According to others, Sirko was born in a Cossack settlement of Merefa, Sloboda, Ukraine (now the Kharkiv region). Legend has it that the birth of Ivan Sirko was already unusual - the boy was born with teeth, which frightened everyone present! His father tried to remedy the situation by saying that Ivan "would gnaw his enemies with his teeth". But this did little to calm the villagers. The child was treated with apprehension, and to some extent, this was justified because he had exhibited unusual abilities from childhood, which later became simply supernatural.

Ivan Sirko, an extremely talented warrior and an outstanding politician of his time, made about 50 military campaigns and suffered no defeat.

Just take part in the French-Spanish Thirty Years' War (1618-1648) on the side of the French! In 1646, in a treaty with the French, signed by Bohdan Khmelnytskyi, 2,500 Cossacks reached the French port of Calais by sea via Gdańsk. The Cossacks were led by Colonels Sirko and Soltenko. It was thanks to the military skill of the Cossacks that they managed to take the impregnable fortress of Dunkirk, which was in the hands of the Spaniards.

The fortress was of great strategic importance - it was called 'the key to the English Channel'. The French repeatedly tried to take Dunkirk but in vain. And the Cossacks took the fortress in a few days and, in fact, handed the French the coveted "key". Sirko also fought against the Turkish Sultan, gaining numerous glorious victories. It was not in vain that the Turks and Tatars called Sirko the Urus-Shaitan and the seven-headed dragon. A famous letter to the Turkish Sultan Muhammad IV was signed in the name of the legendary ataman - the one that was immortalized in a painting by Ilya Repin! The authority of Ivan Sirko in the Cossacks was enormous.

Cossacks of Zaporizhzhia elected him ataman 12 times - from 1659 to August 1680, i.e., until his death.

These are pretty real, though surprising, facts. But about Sirk was said the most incredible things. That neither a bullet nor a sword could touch him, for example. That Sirko was a werewolf who could turn into a wolf! And that he was a "great character". But who are such characterists? So, in Zaporizhzhya, Sich called people who today would be called magicians or psychics. They possessed supernatural abilities. Cossacks who had secret knowledge were ascribed different skills: finding and hiding treasures, curing wounds, and, what was unbelievable, "raising the dead on their feet, and being transferred from one side of the steppe to the other in a moment". Characterists were believed to be able to turn into wolves. In pre-Christian times, the god-thunderer was pictured accompanied by two wolves or greyhounds. The transformation into a hort (wolf) is mentioned in the legends about ataman Sirko. Not without reason, the word 'Sirko' is one of the epithets of the wolf. It is also no coincidence that the name of the island of Khortitsa comes from the word 'hort'.

There are legends in which a Cossack turns into a beast to get to the other world and bring a dying or just deceased comrade back to life. It was believed that this could only be done in the guise of a wolf. It was also said that the men of character possessed the art of hypnotism. How else can one explain the stories of how they cast a "ghost" on their enemies?

The stories about the Cossacks often mention the cases when superior enemy forces attacked a Cossack detachment, and the enemy 'hid'. To do that, the Cossacks quickly poked stakes around the Cossack detachment to create a fence.

The characteristics gave the impression to the enemy that the forest in front of them was an ordinary grove. And the "deceived" enemies would pass by. But sometimes they were less fortunate: using magic spells, the characterists could make their enemies slit each other's throats! Even the elements were subject to them! Fire, water, earth, and air were at their command. They were said to be able to disperse clouds, bring thunder or, conversely, calm the stirring elements.

Therefore it is not surprising that the saying used to be: "A Cossack from Zaporizhzhya can outwit the devil himself".

Many Cossack hetmans, Stake Atamans, and colonels were considered characterists: Dmitry Baida-Vishnevetsky, Ivan Pidkova, Samoilo Kishka, Ivan Bogun, Severin Nalyvaiko, Maxim Krivonos.

They say that Ivan Bogun once led an army through a Polish camp at night, and not a single dog barked!

But the most famous and influential character was ataman Ivan Sirko. Koshevoy Sirko was a great sorcerer. It was not without reason that the Turks nicknamed him Shaitan.

The Cossacks said that Sirko was unique in the world. They said that when he put his hand to a sword strike, only a blue trace was left on it. Sirko could put his enemies to sleep, often turning into a white hound.

But Sirko not only defeated people, he also defeated evil forces. The river Chertomlyk was so named because Sirko killed a devil in it: he only flashed his feet when Sirko fired a pistol at him.

Not only was Ivan Sirko's earthly life turbulent, but also his posthumous life. The great character warrior continued to defeat his enemies even after his death! He bequeathed to the Cossacks to cut off his right hand after his death and march with it.

The Cossacks carried out the ataman's behest and, meeting the enemy, put his hand forward with the words: "Sirk's soul and hand are with us!" The Cossacks believed: that where the hand, there was luck. Therefore Cossacks were feared by Turks and Poles for a long time. In one legend, Sirko was even called Sirentiy the Right-Handed. The hand of Koshevoy was buried only after the destruction of Zaporizhzhya Sich.

And on Sirko's grave, there was an inscription on the cross: "Whoever during seven years before Easter takes three handfuls of earth on my grave will have the same power as I do and will know as much as I do."

Also alive is the incredible legend that Ivan Sirko's hand helped defeat the French in the War of 1812. When the Russian army was at Borodino, Cossack Mikhailo Nelipa told Field Marshal Kutuzov about Ataman Sirko's victorious right hand. The thing is that Nelipa's family had been taking care of the ataman's remains for generations. And, on reflection, Kutuzov sent Cossacks to fetch the hand.

But Nelipa's grandfather, the old keeper of Zaporizhzhia ataman's remains, did not agree to give him his hand for nothing! The Cossacks begged him for a long time, but finally, they managed to persuade him. Old Nelipa yielded his hand only under Field Marshal Kutuzov's guarantee.

The hand was wrapped three times around the French-occupied Moscow, and... the French withdrew from the Russian capital. The fate of the war was decided. That's how Ivan Sirko helped the Russian army defeat the French. Don't you believe it? Does this story seem unbelievable to you? But after the war, in 1813, Kutuzov petitioned to bury the remains of Ivan Sirko. Why would he worry about some long-dead Cossack from Zaporizhzhia? The petition was satisfied, and Sirko's remains were buried in 1836 on the outskirts of village Kapulovka of Nikopol district.

Ivan Sirko's grave suffered back in 1709 during the devastation of Chertomlytsya Sich. But locals saved it, and Cossack families have been looking after the ataman's grave for generations.

In November 1967, when the Koshov ataman's grave was washed away by the waves of Kakhovskoye Reservoir, the ataman's remains were reburied. But before that, the ataman's skull was removed from the grave under extraordinary circumstances.

As Ivan Sirko was solemnly buried with a great gathering of people for the second time, it was impossible to bury him decapitated. A solution was found easily: another skull was put in the coffin during the excavations of the same barrow.

Ataman's skull was sent to Moscow to produce a sculptural portrait for the anthropological reconstruction of Ivan Sirko's appearance.

After that, Sirko's skull remained in Moscow for almost a quarter of a century. It was brought back only in 1990, before celebrating the 500th anniversary of the Ukrainian Cossacks. But even that was not the end of the wanderings. After the anniversary celebration, Ivan Sirko's skull ended up in the safe of the head of the local culture department, where it had been kept for another seven years until it was passed to the Dniprovsky Historical Museum.

In the summer of 2000, after numerous appeals from historians, it was decided to bury the skull of Ataman Ivan Sirko together with the other remains in the mound of Baba Grave. And 320 years after his death, the famous ataman has finally found peace and rest.

Interesting Facts About the Motherland Statue in Kiev

The statue of the Mother Motherland is located in Kyiv, on the bank of the Dnieper River, and attracts attention with its grandeur. The figure of the Mother Motherland is considered to be one of the tallest statues in the world. The statue was unveiled on May 9, 1981.

● The statue's height is 102 meters, and the figure's height from the pedestal to the tip of the sword is 62 meters.

● The statue holds a 16-meter sword weighing 9 tonnes and a shield weighing 13 tonnes. The entire structure weighs 450 tonnes.

The foremost sculptor is Vasily Boroday. The sculptor Galina Kalchenko, a colleague of Boroday's, was the prototype for the statue's face.

The metal frame of the statue is made of stainless steel. Sheets 50 by 50 centimeters in size and one and a half millimeters thick were made in Zaporizhzhia. If you add up the length of all seams of the monument, you get about thirty kilometers.

The sword of the Kyiv sculpture is three-dimensional, diamond-shaped. A pendulum damping the vibrations is installed inside for stability.

● Every year, the Motherland is subjected to a strict inspection. According to specialists, the monument can stand for more than 150 years and withstand a 9-point earthquake.

There are two lifts inside the monument, one inclined and one vertical. The first goes up into the pedestal, the second takes you to the statue's chest, then up the stairs to the arms and head, where the viewing platforms are located. To climb the Motherland Monument in Kyiv, you must buy an entrance ticket.

All sightseers are supervised. Older people, pregnant women, and children under the age of twelve are not allowed up the stairs as they have to climb the stairs for part of the way up.

The monument was assembled using a special 100-meter crane, which was later dismantled.

Legend has it that during the construction of the monument, the Metropolitan of Kyiv had a vision that the sword must not be raised above the cross of the nearby bell tower of the Kyiv-Pechersk Lavra. Therefore, the height of the monument was reduced to 102 m. The original plan was 108 m.

Ukrainian Cuisine

What You Didn't Know About the Famous Ukrainian Dish
Borscht

B orscht is a trademark of Ukrainian national cuisine. This dish has become so popular during the centuries of its existence that almost all neighboring nations want to take "copyright" to it.

However, historical records from the distant past confirm that it was on Ukrainian soil borsch first began to be cooked.

Here are a few interesting facts about the main dish of Ukrainian cuisine:

- In ancient times, it was believed that the deceased's soul flew to Heaven with the steam from the borsch. Therefore, the funeral dinner without this dish is usual.

There are over 70 recipes for red borsch. The most expensive recipe is "Kyiv borsch." It is cooked in a broth of beef, lamb, and pork. In addition to the ingredients, you will also add natural bread kvass.

- According to the classic Ukrainian recipe, borsch is flavored with fresh pork fat at the end of cooking time and pounded with garlic, salt, and herbs. After that, the dish is taken off the fire, covered with a lid, and left to infuse for at least half an hour.

- Poltava region cooks borscht based on chicken broth. It is served with dumplings.

- In the Chernihiv region, traditional borsch is served with mushroom "ushka".

- Zhytomyr region has two variants of borsch: Polesski and Korostenski. The first one is cooked with dried loaches and mushrooms, the second - with dried fruit.

- Zakarpattya region has not managed to find its recipe for borsch. The region cooks so-called Lvovsky. They do not add cabbage to it - only potatoes and beets are cooked.

- In ancient times, borsch in Galicia was cooked very liquid. Potatoes were not added. To make it sour, they added cherry or apple juice.

- Jewish people cook borscht with chicken broth and a lot of sugar. The beets are not stewed beforehand.

- Ukrainians began to add tomato dressing to borscht only in the late XIX - early XX century: before that, tomatoes were not ordinary in Ukraine. Earlier, the sourness was added with whey, sour milk, sauerkraut, berries, or unripe apples.

- The unofficial "borsch index" (similar to the "Big Mac index") is often used by the Ukrainian media to assess the purchasing power of various currencies and determine the actual inflation of the Ukrainian hryvnia. The borsch index is the average cost of all products needed to cook a certain amount of the dish at a specific date.

- A small town Borshchev in the Ternopil region, is named after the borsch. Every autumn there is a festival, "Borscht". Guests are offered not only to try but also to learn how to cook different kinds of borsch.

Why is a Ukrainian Chicken Cutlet Called a «Chicken Kiev»?

Chicken Kyiv cutlet is a kind of cutlet in the form of a chopped chicken fillet wrapped with a piece of cold butter. It is fried in a deep fryer and covered in beaten-up egg and breadcrumbs. Grated cheese, mushrooms, herbs, egg yolk and other ingredients can be added to the butter.

The French cutlet (Côtelettes de volaille) is often confused with the Ukrainian version of the dish, and it is no accident. They contain similar ingredients: chicken breast with stuffing. Only the Ukrainian version uses butter as a stuffing, and a little spice - herbs, pepper, and egg yolk - is added to it. If you add more seasoning and sauce instead of butter (or do without it), it is the French 'Côtelettes de volaille'.

Kyiv started to cook similar cutlets during the reign of hetman Pavlo Skoropadsky (1918). They were supposedly served to the officers of the Hetman's headquarters in the restaurant of the "Continental" hotel. The dish was called "Kyiv-style cutlet de vole". But due to the difficult economic and military situation, the plate did not take root among the people.

There is another version, an American one. The dish is believed to have been brought by Ukrainian immigrants, who opened restaurants in the U.S.

In the Chicago Tribune in 1937, Colonel Vladimir Yashchenko, owner of the Yar restaurant in Chicago, recalls a dish called "chicken breast cooked chicken Kyiv-style". Yashchenko studied in Petrograd, served in the Russian Imperial Army, and came to Chicago in 1926.

In 1947, this dish began a new life in Ukraine, thanks to an occasion once again connected with France. A Ukrainian delegation was returning from Paris, where a number of peace treaties had been signed with former German satellites of the last war (after all, Ukraine was a founding member of the United Nations). The delegates celebrated their return with a reception, at which they were served chicken cutlets stuffed with butter. The republic's leadership liked the new dish very much, so it soon appeared in the restaurant "Chicken Kyiv cutlets".

According to one of the versions, the dish's name is attributed to Nikita Khrushchev. Once at the meeting, he remembered "Kyiv cutlets" because he had been treated to them in Kyiv. The name stuck.

It is also believed that Ukraine invented to leave the bone in the cutlets. They put a paper clip on the last one, and it was convenient to eat the cutlet with your hands.

In the early '60s, Chicken Kyiv cutlets were sold to the public, spreading in the restaurant and culinary systems. Unfortunately, it began to "degrade" - less and less remained of the original recipe. The meat of the soon-to-be-ripened broilers is being replaced by domestic chicken, considerably inferior in taste. The quality butter was replaced by sandwich butter, melted cheese, and, in culinary versions, filling of unknown composition.

Interesting facts

Sometimes, curiosities happen while eating Chicken Kyiv cutlets. But, most often - with foreigners, who, unaware of the unusual stuffing, trying to cut the cutlet with a knife, were sprinkled with a trickle of oil. Therefore, in high-level restaurants, the "Chicken Kyiv" dish is accompanied by a special instruction: "Beware! The cutlet shoots!".

George Bush's speech on August 1, 1991, in Kyiv, in which he called on Ukrainians to stay within the USSR, went down in history as "Chicken Kyiv" (chicken Kyiv cutlet) because in English, the word "chicken" means "coward".

Chicken Kyiv cutlets are so famous that in 2006 they were included in the U.K. consumer basket. And in cities in the US, Germany, and Canada, where Ukrainians live, many restaurants offer Chicken Kyiv as a specialty.

Ukrainian Holiday Celebrations

Why do Ukrainians Celebrate Two "New Years"?

U krainians celebrate New Year's Eve twice: on 1 and 14 January (Old and New Style), and the name 'Old New Year' never ceases to amaze foreigners.

The thing is that in the Russian Empire, to which part of modern Ukraine belonged, they used to live according to the Julian calendar (introduced by the Roman emperor Gaius Julius Caesar in late 46 BC - the so-called 'old style'). But the year, according to the Julian calendar, didn't coincide with the solar calendar and was longer by 6 hours. And so, Pope 1583 introduced the Gregorian calendar - the current international standard (new style). The dates were "shifted", but the Orthodox Church rejected the Gregorian calendar because it did not conform to the canonical rules for celebrating Easter and determining its date.

That is why Christmas and New Year's Day did not coincide either! In 1918 the Soviet regime approved the adoption of the Gregorian calendar, which was accepted worldwide. But the Ukrainian Orthodox Church still lives according to the Julian calendar, with Christmas on January 7. Until then, the faithful continue to fast, so they avoid the lavish Christmas feast of January 1. Ukraine is a multicultural country. On the other hand, Western Ukraine Catholics celebrate Christmas on December 25 and New Year on January 1, by which time all restrictions on food are lifted.

Ukrainian Easter Egg

The history of the Easter egg as a phenomenon begins in the distant past, from the pagan cult. It was an essential element of a variety of rituals and ceremonies. Paschanka is closely linked to the religious beliefs of distant ancestors about the creation of the world, with fertility and worship, with solemn rituals associated with the annual cycle of nature's revival and praise of its forces. The egg is a symbol of the beginning, new life, and rebirth; such meaning was known to all peoples in ancient times, so it remains today. The drawings of old egg paintings repeat the motifs of painted pottery of Trypillya culture. Thus, researchers distinguish between prehistoric tombs of Slavic and non-Slavic; the use and manufacture of urinal designs were characteristic of the ethnic groups of the Slavs, who later were called Ukrainians.

In antiquity, in the days before the adoption of Christianity, Easter eggs served as a talisman for its owner. The small balls were put in the middle of ceramic eggs, knocked during the shaking, and chased away by the sound of evil spirits and evil forces. Archaeologists found such Easter eggs in burials in Novgorod and Kyiv. These first cities were the centers of the art of painting

Easter eggs during Kievan Rus. In total, archeologists found about 20 cities on the territory of our country, where the art of producing similar amulets was spread.

According to the beliefs of their distant Ukrainian ancestors, pysanka had good magical powers - it brought happiness, prosperity, and well-being and protected its owner from evil forces. Sometimes pysanka was buried under the ground so that the egg would make the harvest rich and generous. They were placed on the graves of their ancestors, set in the middle of the graves of young children, and lovers used Easter eggs to express their feelings. People regarded it as an artist painting the egg so that it would become a genuine amulet so that the symbolism depicted on it performed its essential function. To do this, one must know when to start making egg parchment, how to pray beforehand, and to whom exactly egg parchment will be given as a gift.

Time has passed, and the symbolism has lost its deeply sacred meaning. Only the connection between children's games and the holiday of Easter remained. Pagan symbols acquired a different interpretation and meaning, gradually merging with Christian motifs.

The process of making Easter eggs is not simple. In ancient times it was influenced by many factors. One had to paint Eggs in clearly defined hours, having previously completed a plot, and signs and symbols were painted in appropriate colors. Nowadays, only the symbolism of colors and images has remained significant in this variety of conditions. The technique of making egg pysanka divided all eggs into twenty types, but only five have survived until today.

The most famous motifs of ornaments in Easter eggs (which used to be more than a hundred):

* Krivulka, or infinity - signifies the eternal movement of the sun, the thread of life.

Rose, Trigver, star, and square cross are symbols of the sun, signifying the four sides of the world. Trigver (otherwise known as training, has existed in culture since the time of the Tripole) - means the symbols of life: earth, sky and air, and fire, air, and water.

- Forty wedges represent forty points in life, prosperity, and success in the household, a person's wealth, and decency.

* The spider or rosettes, mills, and spider's web are the oldest solar sign. The dots represent the tears of the Mother of God, the heavenly lights.

* Plants, spruce branches - Youth in its eternity, health, the vitality of nature, beauty.

* Spikes of wheat-the harvest.

Eggs colored in the same color are called Easter eggs. The color of an egg also carries a particular meaning.

Red means life, joy, hope, and love, and for the unmarried, it means marriage and finding a mate.

Yellow represents the moon, the stars in the household denoting the harvest.

Blue is associated with the sky and the air; its magical meaning is health.

Green represents the resurrection, rebirth of nature, richness and bounty, fertility, and abundant harvest.

The combination of black and white colors speaks of respect for the dead souls, thus expressing gratitude for their help and protection from evil spells.

A combination of several colors in patterns (four or five colors) means happiness in family, peace, love, success, and prosperity.

Each area has its preferences in color, which can determine the origin of eggs. Masters of Polissya, Volyn, and partly Podolia make their eggs primarily red. In the Sub-Dniester region, they put patterns in broad symmetric fields and thick lines on eggs. In Nadnistria, dark or white backgrounds on dark pheasant eggs are typical. Boikovsky Easter eggs have two colors; Hutsuls ones are distinguished by being painted in yellow and white red.

The gift of Easter eggs was full of deep meaning, made with the desire to bring good, help, or even charm. Easter eggs given to small children were of light colors; guys and girls were offered eggs with solar symbols and triggers made in cheerful colors. Homemakers usually received forty Ukrainian easter egg wedges and zigzags, and the elderly - with belts in red tones.

The technology of making Ukrainian Easter eggs also varied. The most common way of painting eggs was scribbling, when the melted wax was poured into a scribbler (a specific variation of a pen for writing), made of thin tin, and then the egg was dipped into the paint of a particular color. Places covered with wax would subsequently remain white. Then they waxed up the places where they planned to make a new pattern and again dipped it in paint of another color, and so on several times. When all planned lines, signs, and ornaments were done, an egg was heated; as a rule, it was done in a cooker, where wax melted and flowed down. So remained multicolored and, each time, uniquely original ornaments.

There are legends about Easter eggs; some have survived until today. One of them, for example, says that the fate of the whole world depends on the number of Eggs that are painted annually. As long as the Eggs are made, the world is safe, but as soon as the custom is forgotten or ignored, the devil is released from the iron fetters by which he is now immobilized, and the world is destroyed. The devil lives underground, and an iron chain chains him to the rock. And every year, he sends his acolytes on a journey around the world to see with their eyes if they are still writing scribes or if many are still being made. If there are still many, the bonds remain strong, and the devil's power is less, for human love is above all, and no evil can resist it. Therefore, the more everyone makes a Paschanka, the more love and goodness will reign in the world. And the days before Easter are an incentive to create beautifully painted eggs with wishes of excellence, health, and prosperity for their families and loved ones.

Celebrating Christmas in Ukraine: Main Traditions and Symbols

Ukrainians celebrate Christmas according to different calendars: the Gregorian calendar (December 25) and the Julian calendar (January 7). Most Ukrainians prefer the January calendar.

There are many different traditions and rituals associated with Christmas. Here are the main rules for celebrating Christmas in Ukraine:

Lent. About 40 days before Christmas begins the Nativity Fast, one of the longest in the year. It is not at the top by strictness, but it lasts 40 days and is necessary to purify the body and soul before Christmas. During the Advent, fast any fruits and vegetables, porridges, beans, mushrooms, and on most days of the fast, fish can be eaten. No meat, eggs, cheese, dairy products, or butter may be eaten during Lent.

Holy evening. On January 6, people traditionally celebrate the Holy Evening, an obligatory attribute of 12 fasting dishes on the table. There are two interpretations of this number: according to one, it is the number of apostles, and according to another, it is the number of months in one year.

Kutya. The main dish of the evening is kutya (boiled wheat mixed with poppy seeds, honey, walnuts, and sultanas). And after the feast with the family, it is customary to take the dinner to the godparents. They take kutya and other dishes and visit them for a few hours, but then they must return home to spend Christmas morning with their families. In the afternoon, they visit grandparents who live apart or other relatives.

Didukh. The main decoration of the house is the didukh, a bundle of wheat stalks symbolizing the ancestors' spirit, wealth, prosperity, and the family's talisman. On these holy days, the ancestors are believed to return to spend time with their families. The Didukh is placed in the most honorable place in the house - under the images.

Carols. From the evening of January 6, it is customary to have a big star in their hands: carolers sing Christmas carols. Boys and girls prepare memorable songs and poems they sing from house to house, entertaining their neighbors in exchange for sweet gifts and coins. It is believed that the more carolers come to the house, the more wealth and prosperity the family will have during the following year.

Fortune-telling. The tradition of fortune-telling on Christmas Eve is even older than Christmas in Ukraine. Many people think that one shouldn't read fortune on this day, and others, on the contrary, believe in the magic power of the holiday and that fortune-telling on Christmas Eve can help find out the future. Girls in Ukraine will still read their fortune today to find out if they will marry and the name of the future groom. January 6-7 are also considered prophetic dreams.

The morning of January 7 begins with people greeting each other with the phrase "Christ is born!" and the response "Praise Him!" People attend church for Christmas prayer and gather with their families on this day. On this day, people no longer limit themselves to a fasting meal.

Feast of Vasiliy and Malanka

January 13 is celebrated on the feast of Malanka (other names are Melanka, Malania) or Generous Evening, also called Vasiliev Evening. This is a Ukrainian folk and church holiday, the evening before the "old" New Year or St. Vasiliy the Great, i.e., on January 13, they celebrate: the holiday of Malanka, Shchedriven Evening, and Vasiliev Evening, and on January 14 - St. Vasiliy and the Old New Year.

January 13 is called St. Vasiliev evening, Vasiliev's carol, Fat Kutya, Shchedriy evening, and Shchedrukha. The holiday takes its name from St. Basil the Great, who is considered the patron of pigs and the protector of gardens from worms. That is why the date of January 14 was also called a pig feast. There was a ritual dish on every table - "Caesarean pig". The dish was named after Saint Basil, Archbishop of Caesarea of Cappadocia, who was popularly nicknamed Caesarea.

On the eve of St. Vasiliy's Day, which is celebrated on January 14 in Ukraine, it is customary to show a bounty. On holiday, it is common to make a generous kutya and make fortune-telling. According to omens, on this day at home, one must have enough money and not lend money. Homemakers baked biscuits in the form of poultry or cattle. Many people had pork dishes on the table. Every family member tried to get up earlier in the morning and go to the well, spring, or river, draw water and wash with it. It was believed that the one who did this would stay healthy and in good spirits for the whole year.

The custom of driving Vasiliy's goat on January 13/14 is a mystical act that dates back to pre-Christian times. The goat was made from a wooden stick, one end of which was split into horns. The horns were decorated with wooden spoons - goat ears. On the side of the stick, a goat's tail was hooked and dressed in an old sheepskin coat with its fur on top. The coat sleeves would hang down - these were the goat's 'legs'.

How to drive a goat: Scenario for the feast

The chosen "goat" gets under the cape, holds the decorated stick with one hand, and turns its "tail".

In addition to the goat, the company chooses a "cat" for the evening - usually the youngest guy in the group. The "cat" is responsible for carrying the bag, meowing, and asking for lard.

►The activity begins as darkness falls. The children approach any hut and ask: "let me into the house because the goat is so cold!

The owner refuses three times, and the children ask again.

►After this, the "goat" and the bounty hunters sing, and the cat meows and asks for lard. During this time, the goat supposedly dies and comes back to life.

►After three traditional refusals, the hostess still treats the cat to lard, the goat-herder to pie, and the group treasurer to money.

► Having fun, the youngsters gather in the same house and continue to party.

Who is Malanka, and how is it Celebrated in Ukraine?

Malanka is a Ukrainian folk and church holiday associated with the feast day of Venerable Melania. Melanka-Woda and Vasiliy-month come on the Big Night to inform the hosts about the upcoming holidays and celebrate the guests called Melanka's guests by the people.

According to church traditions, January 13 is the day of Venerable Melania (IV-Vth century). Melania was born into a Christian family, very wealthy and respected. When she was 14, she was given in marriage to Apinianus, who was also from a noble family. This young family used all their possessions to help those in need. After many years of godly deeds, Melania settled on the Mount of Olives, and later a monastery was founded there. The Venerable

Melania had two children. The second birth was complicated, and the boy soon died. That is why the saint is often prayed for in difficult childbirths.

The mock wedding of Melania and Basil was often acted out. Melania's groom's name was not chosen by chance, as her day was followed by the day of memory of Basil of Caesarea, which opened the new year. So, Melan's wedding is a symbolic meeting of the old and new year, with wishes for the harvest and happiness in the coming year.

The scenario of the Malanka Feast

On Malanka Day, Ukrainians play Melanka to spend the Old Year as cheerfully as possible:

The guy who knows how to joke best is chosen from a group of young people. He dresses up and becomes "Melanka".

Others also dress up as gypsies, bears, cranes, or devils, whichever is the most interesting.

This can also be done in the daytime - the children run after the dressed-up fancy-dressers in droves.

The kids do not go to every house, but only those where they can meet the girls. As with goat-driving, permission to cheer must be requested in song form.

The landlord invites the whole family into the house to watch the merrymakers, especially the girls.

The "Melanka" walks around the house and does harm: she may scatter rubbish or move dishes. The homemakers know this custom, so they close their eyes on Melanka to ensure she does not touch anything.

The lads are generous, making fun of the bad homemakers. The girls laugh and praise the song and dance. Each merrymaker displays his abilities by dancing to his heart's content.

When the Shchodnik is finally over, everyone sits at the festive table. Melanka is chosen as a girl, but she is more respectful and stately; she is dressed up as a young woman. The girls, being generous, do not enter the house but stand under the windows and sing.

Ukrainian Traditions and Arts

Ukrainian Trembita - the World's Most Extended Musical Instrument

U kraine has always been famous for the diversity of its music. Therefore, it is not surprising that Ukrainians have created many musical instruments, among which the trembita occupies a special place.

Trembita is a musical instrument of mountain Ukrainians, also known as Hutsuls. The instrument is home to the soul of the Ukrainian mountains. Trembita is the most extended instrument globally; its length varies from 3 to 8 meters. The sound range of the trembita reaches 2.5 octaves, and the sound can travel more than 10 kilometers.

The trembita has made the Guinness Book of World Records. Ukrainian Hutsuls used to live their lives to the sound of the trembita. It was used to announce the going out of sheep to pasture, the passing of a child, or the birth of a family. They were invited to weddings and caroled with it.

For the shepherd, the Trembita is not just a musical instrument. It used to be the shepherd's only means of communication with the village, an old mobile phone. They were used to tell the time, and the most experienced shepherds were even able to predict the weather. It is said that the tool can sense rain and thunderstorms particularly well.

Although Trembita looks simple, it is a deceptive impression. It often takes two years to make. First, one must choose a good spruce, preferably a thunderbird. That is a tree that has been struck by lightning. The Hutsuls are convinced that the voice of the Creator is transmitted to the tree by celestial thunder. The cut tree is left to harden for a year.

And only after that comes the most crucial moment. It has to be split in half with one blow, and the core has to be chiseled by hand - this can take a year. And the final step is to bark the two halves together. It would seem that it is not easy to hold a several-meter-long instrument and play it simultaneously. A three-meter-long trembita weighs no more than one and a half kilograms.

Vyshyvanka - the National Clothing of Ukrainians

Ukrainian embroidered shawl is often called the nation's code with encrypted amulets, symbols, and signs. Details and themes of the embroidery pattern vary depending on the historical region of Ukraine.

Masters talk about embroidery as a process of uplift and spiritual growth: a

Ukrainian woman has invested in the beauty and subtle spiritual symbolism, laying the signs of the region and her family.

Ukrainian embroidery has a long history, as evidenced by the first excavations of Trypillya culture (elements of ornaments Ukrainian embroidery adorned pottery of that time). Later, it was found that the Scythians wore embroidered clothes.

Traditionally, the most common color of fabrics in the Ukrainian embroidery shirt is white, which symbolizes purity, tenderness, and pristine. Black on the Ukrainian embroidered shirts has traditionally been the color of dissatisfaction and sadness.

At all times, the handiwork was appreciated, so hand-embroidered vestments are precious work which contributes to the master embroidering the ornament. Embroidery ornaments are divided into three main groups:

- Abstract (geometric) ornament.

- Plant ornament.

- Animal ornament

The animal ornament can now be found not only in the embroidery and in the collections of famous designers, inspired by the culture and traditional costumes of the Ukrainian people.

It is charming to see that even foreign celebrities wear blouses in the style of Ukrainian embroidery.

In terms of color scheme, the classic embroidery blouse is white but also can be divided into three groups: one-color, two-color, and multi-color.

Mono-colored embroideries look very unusual, often in a light color - white or cream. The pattern is mostly embroidered with silk threads. Such embroidered vans are popular in Chernihiv and Poltava regions.

Two-colored embroidered vestments were most common in the Kyiv and Vinnytsia regions. Mainly red threads were used for the embroidery ornaments, which were sometimes supplemented with a black line to highlight the pattern.

Multicolored embroideries are typical for the Carpathians, Transcarpathian, and Hutsul regions. Here mostly vegetable ornaments were used.

Each color has its meaning, as embroidery is traditionally considered a talisman for its owner. The first baby was embroidered from the cloth and trimmed with candles at the baptism of the godparents. This embroidery guarded the child against bad luck and everything wrong; in some areas, even embroidered on an inconspicuous part of the embroidery red cross.

The colors of the patterns carry this secret meaning:

- White - served as protection from evil forces. Young girls chose this embroidery to emphasize their natural beauty.

- Black was the color of sadness and pessimism and was often chosen for the deceased and the bereaved.

- Red is the color for good luck and protection.

* Yellow is the color of wealth and prosperity and symbolizes the sun as the energy for all life.

- Green is the color of birth and growth.

In our time, embroideries are made of different fabrics and techniques. In addition to cross or plain embroidery, embroidery patterns are embroidered with beads. This variant is suitable in the first place for women's embroidery. The print looks volume.

Interesting facts about the Ukrainian embroidery:

* Vyshyvanka is festive, not everyday clothing. On weekdays Ukrainians wore the so-called "budenki" - inconspicuous shirts, and on holidays they wore richly embroidered shirts.

- Embroidery was applied primarily with a sacred purpose, as a talisman, protecting the parts of the body not covered by clothes. Some embroidered shirts were originally created as a ritual.

- Each region of Ukraine has its embroidery technique, ornament, and traditional embroidery colors. Sometimes even individual villages can boast their unique embroidery.

* In the past, the embroidery was an exclusively female activity. Traditionally, a girl would fast, pray, and wash her hands before embroidering. Nowadays, not only women embroider, but also men.

- Embroidering a single shirt can take from two weeks to three years - depending on the complexity of the techniques.

- Excellent embroidery 'white on white' was popular among European nobles and Ukrainian nobles, who wore embroidered underwear and body shirts.

- Nowadays, researchers of embroidery count more than 200 ancient stitches based on 20 embroidery techniques: ironing, spike stitch, knotwork, lace, twisted stitch, cutting, pecking, goatskin, plaiting, and tracery.

- Poppies, which are popular today as an element of the pattern, were practically not used in traditional Ukrainian embroidery because they symbolized sorrow and death and were widely used at the end of the XX century.

* The first fashionista, who combined Ukrainian embroidery with everyday clothes, was a Ukrainian poet and writer Ivan Franko. He stylishly combined an embroidered shirt with a jacket. The writer can be seen wearing the 20 grivnas banknote.

Ukrainian embroidery ornaments have recently been used to decorate shirts, cars, and household items and are used as patterns for tattoos and manicures.

Ukrainian Wedding Traditions

A traditional Ukrainian wedding has always been distinguished by its splendor, solemnity, colorfulness, and beautiful wedding traditions.

There are a lot of such traditions, all of which are interesting and original in their way, and most are very actual, even at modern Ukrainian weddings.

Matchmaking

In the past, the road to marriage started with matchmaking. With the headmen, the boy went to the girl he wanted to marry. If the girl gave her consent, they entered into a marriage ceremony. Nowadays, the matchmaking ceremony is rather conventional, but various traditional rites often accompany it.

Matchmakers are significant participants in wedding ceremonies. They act as official witnesses of the marriage and participate actively in all wedding ceremonies. They are usually made up of family members or godparents, one from each side. In the past, they also acted as matchmakers.

The loaf is an important attribute that should be present at every Ukrainian wedding. It is decorated with traditional dough ornaments. Previously, it also acted as a wedding cake, but both are usually present at modern weddings. During the blessing ceremony, one of the parents holds the loaf as a symbol of the unity of the two families.

Engagement

Engagement is the first ceremony before a wedding, which takes place immediately after the marriage agreement and is accompanied by a loud celebration in honor of the couple. Both families are seated at a table, and the eldest man wraps a towel around the newlyweds' hands. It is customary for the newlyweds to present everyone present with a handkerchief then.

The newlyweds are then considered engaged and may not refuse to marry. In the past, if someone wanted to avoid getting married after the engagement, he or she was considered dishonorable and had to pay the other family for the insult.

The ransom

Another somewhat old tradition is the bride price. In the old days, the groom could buy back his bride from his parents for money or any valuables, but now this tradition is joking. During the redemption ceremony, the bridegroom or her friends must perform various tasks from the bride's relatives or "redeem" the bride in exchange for vodka.

The blessing

Before going to church, the newlyweds traditionally ask their parents for their blessing for the marriage. At the bride's house, they kneel on an embroidered towel. The elders are present to hold the icons. The parents give their children their blessings and wish them a happy married life.

Getting married

The young couple enters the church as equals, hand in hand. Before the ceremony begins, they should tell the priest they are getting married of their own free will. The priest then leads the couple down the aisle, symbolizing God directing the young couple into marriage.

Rings in a wedding ceremony symbolize that the woman is no longer free but belongs to her man. This symbol of fidelity is blessed by the priest and placed in the couple's hands before they are ushered down the aisle.

The embroidered towel is essential in wedding traditions. They wrap icons around it and accompany the newlyweds from the blessing to the wedding, where they stand on it to enter into marriage.

This means that they will never stand on bare ground" - to live in poverty. It is believed that the first to stand on the towel will be the head of the family. Their hands are tied with an embroidered towel for the ceremony to show that the newlyweds are one.

The priest then circles the couple around the small altar three times as a sign that marriage is a journey led by Jesus Christ. Now the young couple is no longer just boyfriend and girlfriend; they become married and take three sips of wine from the same silver cup as a symbol that everything in marriage - both sorrow and joy - will be shared by the two.

The candles at the wedding ceremony act as a symbol that marriage is a spiritual event, and Christ is the light that illuminates the beginning of the new life of the newlyweds. The bride and groom each hold a candle during the entire ceremony.

The crowns, held above the young couple's heads during the wedding ceremony, symbolize the bride and groom becoming the King and Queen of their family realm, and the crown itself represents the crown of creation.

Crowns can be either gold or wreaths that are woven from miter. They were once worn for a few days after the wedding. In another tradition, at the end of the wedding ceremony, the bride-to-be takes off her wreath and veil and wears a headscarf as a sign that she has entered the statutes of a married woman.

A solemn celebration begins after the wedding ceremony, which lasts for three days according to a long tradition. It is always accompanied by songs, dances, and a sumptuous feast of traditional Ukrainian food.

Popravany (Post-wedding dinner)

Popravany is a concluding tradition of the wedding celebration. On the day after the wedding, it is customary for the bride's parents to treat all the guests to a meal. During this, everyone congratulates the couple on the first day of their married life.

Gopak Fight Dance

Gopak is an old Ukrainian dance that has long been a national dance. The dance dates back to Cossack times, but it has not lost its popularity to this day. It is fun to watch as Gopak is a quick, virtuoso, and stunningly fast dance.

The dance itself reflects the breadth of the Ukrainian soul and has long been a hallmark of Ukrainian culture. Gopak is a dialogue of sorts, where men present their temper, strength, and courage, and girls demonstrate their grace and beauty.

The origin of Gopak is connected with the military training of the Cossacks of Zaporizhzhya Sich in the 16-18 centuries.

Therefore, initially, it was an exclusively male dance. Hetmans, who took mace, started dancing in the center of the circle, and the Cossacks entering the ring confirmed their supremacy. The name gopak came from the word 'gopal' - to jump, and from a similar exclamation 'gop'.

The new history of Gopak began in 1940 with the creation of the Ukrainian Song and Dance Ensemble, which Pavlo Pavlovich Virskyi led from 1955 to 1975. It was the choreographer who created an academic folk dance based on classical and traditional folklore and put the famous Gopak, which the Ukrainian Academic Dance Ensemble named after him, still closes its concerts.

Gopak is a martial dance. Each movement is a kicking fight from different positions, even while sitting. Byzantine historian of the IX century Leo Deacon in "Chronicles", describes the campaigns of Prince Svyatoslav, called magi children of Satan, who learned the art of fighting through dance. The most ancient image of Gopak is ant figures from Kyiv in the 6th century - the so-called Martyniv treasure.

Gopak is a martial dance in which the fighting blows are performed with the feet. It is a so-called all-around defense. When the Cossacks were surrounded, they formed around dance, in which one of them held tightly to the others, and it was almost impossible to tear one out of the circle. And while in the round dance, two men at their sides hold one; the other one tore his legs off the ground and hit the enemy with both feet. This tactic of circular defense is preserved not only in the Cossack gopak but also in the Hutsul harness dance, where it is better seen. Gopak is a dance that is many thousands of years old. The most ancient image of Gopak of warriors from the Kyiv region is from the 6th century A.D.

Over the years, Gopak has degenerated (it loses some of the fighting movements). Without sabers in their hands, these elements of dance are not understandable to most people. The dance becomes immediately understandable if the dancer is given a saber in his hand. The dancer turns into a dangerous warrior who mows enemies with sabers around him by dozens. This trick was used if a Cossack was surrounded. The Cossacks used to cover themselves and then cut their enemies with this movement.

Every movement in the dance was a combat move, a combat strike. The dance was initially called the Cossack.

Even the Cossack formation was ideally suited for Gopak. It was not hot in trousers; besides, it was convenient to stretch, the vest, unlike the kimono, was never untied, and the serpentine belt protected the abdomen and the lower back.

Ukrainian Composer Leontovych Wrote the New Year Song 'Carol of Bells'

The Ukrainian composer Leontovych's New Year's Eve song is sung world-wide. It is about Leontovych's 'Schedryk', one of the most popular New Year's Eve songs. First performed in 1916 in Kyiv, the tune traveled the world and was played at Carnegie Hall in New York in 1921.

"Carol of Bells." Who doesn't know the melody of this song? The tune speaks of the approach of Christmas and creates a festive mood in almost every corner of the globe. When we listen to the "Carol of Bells", we immediately conjure up images of the composer of genius Nikolaj Leontowicz, the author of world-famous choral arrangements of folk songs. Mykola Leontovych is one of the most often performed Ukrainian composers globally, thanks to his "Carol of Bells".

The author was not destined to sit in the front rows of concert halls to hear the triumph of his "Schedryk" performed by the world's pop and film stars. Nikolay Leontovich was killed in the prime of his talent at the age of 44, and it will be 80 years before the truth about his death is known from the archival materials.

And world fame and immortality to the author were brought by his songs. "A Cheerio" has long been a symbol of Christmas in the United States, Canada, Europe, Australia, and even Japan under Carol of The Bells.

The genius of Nikolai Leontovych's 'Schedryk' is that he managed with three notes and four do-si-do sounds to glorify the Ukrainian singing nation across the world. And for more than 100 years, the swallow from "Shchedryk" has been flying around the world.

Now it is difficult to imagine a genre of music that does not include arrangements of Schedryk. Rock bands and rappers perform it, and there are disco and techno versions. "Schedryk" is processed to their taste by representatives of cardinally different musical styles, and every time we have an original, unforgettable version.

In England, "Shchedrik" is called "New Year's serenade"; in Latin America - "the song of the rough sea ", and in Canada - "the newly discovered sphinx". The whole musical world-recognized "Shchedrik" as the song of the XX century and Ukraine - as "the country of songs".

The "Schedryk" was first performed abroad on May 11, 1919, at the National Theatre in Prague. It was their signature number. The choristers gave more than 200 concerts.

Interesting facts about the "Schedryk

The "Shchedrik" has five authors' versions. The composer Nikolaj Leontović dedicated 18 years to it: the first version appeared in 1901, and the last in 1919.

The "Schedryk" was first performed on stage in 1916 by the choir of Kyiv University.

The English version of "Shchedryk" was created in 1936 by Pyotr Olkhovsky, an American of Ukrainian origin.

It was first performed in 1921 on the Carnegie Hall stage in New York in the USA.

"Christmas Hymn of the Bells" (Carol of the Bells) - is the name under which the Ukrainian cheerleader is known.

In Ukraine, there are commemorative coins "Shchedrik" of 5 and 20 hryvnia denomination, launched into circulation by the National Bank of Ukraine.

"The 'Carol of Bells' has been featured in many iconic Hollywood films.

Numerous musicians have created their version of "Shchedrik". Pentatonix became one of those guys. They a cappella sang "Schedrick" in English.

The famous American group, The Piano Guys, recorded their "Carol of Bells" cover. The reworked version of the tune was enormously popular and received hundreds of enthusiastic reactions within weeks.

What Hollywood films have "The Piano Guys" played in:

* Who doesn't remember our "Shchedrik" in the "Home Alone" movie. It is an exciting adaptation of the Ukrainian song "Carol of the Bells".

Ukrainian "Shchedrik" can also be heard in the movie "Two Faces in the Mirror" with Barbra Streisand.

* In the T.V. series "The Mentalist", this song is associated with not-so-happy moments - at the moment when the music is played, Santa dies.

* The English version of "The Cheetah" is also heard in the South Park animated series. It's a bit of a spectacle, "for aficionado", as they say.

The Riddle of Kazimir Malevich's Square

Only two paintings worldwide that even those far from art can recognize unmistakably - Leonardo da Vinci's "La Gioconda" and the "Black Square" by Kazimir Malevich. The author of the latter was born and brought up in Ukraine, and to include him in the pantheon of famous representatives of this country is a matter of discussion even many years after the painter's death.

Malevich has invariably made the list of the most controversial artists. Some people regard him as a genius; their opponents berate the painter for his primitivism and lack of imagination. Although the artist's work is controversial, his contemporaries remember and admire him for his colorful works. Interest in Malevich's personality and canvases has not diminished over time, which is evidence of the artist's crucial historical role.

Kazimir Malevich became a painter in his time to put the main questions before humankind with the help of written paintings. The artist's paintings ask what the future art should be and how best to reflect the essence of things. Malevich asks about what waits for mankind at a point to which infinity tends to reach and how to reach the limit of zero, beyond the intersection of which is the beginning of all things.

Black Square" is Malevich's most exciting and famous work. Here are some interesting facts about the job:

* Not black and not a square. None of the sides of the painting are parallel to any of its other sides or the sides of the square frame framing the creation. As for black, Malevich did not use black at all in this work, and the result was a mixture of colors. In this way, the artist sought to create a dynamic, moving form. "The Black Square is part of a cycle of Suprematist paintings (a movement in avant-garde art founded by Malevich), in which the artist investigated the possibilities of primary color.

- Part of a triptych. As conceived by Malevich, "Black Square" is part of a triptych, which also includes the works "Black Circle" and "Black Cross". They were written for the final futuristic exhibition "0.10" in St. Petersburg, which opened on December 19, 1915. "The Black Square" hung in the "red corner," where it is customary to turn icons.

- Painting Manifesto. In the autumn of 1915, the manifesto of Kazimir Malevich with the famous slogan "from cubism to suprematism" appeared. "The Black Square" the artist declared as "the first step of pure creativity in general". With this work, he demonstrated the new plastic system's main module, Suprematism's style-forming potential.

* The road to the "Black Square". Malevich was prompted to take the path of Suprematism in some way by Mikhail Matyushin's "Victory over the Sun", staged in December 1913. The artist worked on sketches of scenery and costumes for this production. The "black square" image appeared for the first time in those sketches. That was the plastic expression of the victory of active human creativity over the passive form of nature: the black square seemed instead of the solar circle. That's why the artist dated the appearance of the square by 1913, based on the drawings he made during his work on Victory over the Sun. The painting itself was painted in 1915.

* The pinnacle of creativity. "Kazimir Malevich considered the Black Square the pinnacle of his creativity. The artist painted "The Red Square" and "The White Square".

Attractions in Ukraine

Dzhalirgach Island - the Ukrainian Maldives on the Black Sea Coast

Myths and legends have haunted humankind throughout history. According to one such tale, Achilles, son of Thetis, goddess of the sea, fell in love with one of the priestesses of Artemis. Her name was the beautiful Iphigenia. But the priestess did not want to become Achilles' wife and decided to flee to the sea depths to be swallowed by the waves forever. Achilles pursued his beloved, and the goddess Artemis, wishing to save the faithful priestess from death, threw sand under her feet.

This is how the island of Dzharylgach was formed. This magical island is located in the south of Ukraine, on the Karkinit Gulf of the Black Sea. The total length of Dzharylgach is 42 km, of which the island itself is 23 km. Such figures make it the largest island in Ukraine and the Black Sea.

It is unbelievable, but according to many vacationers, the sea on the protected island of Dzharylgach is the same as in the Maldives. This piece of paradise is 30 minutes by sea from Skadovsk in the Kherson region. Amazing white sand beaches, clear blue sea, and clean air.

Dzharylhach is the only European reserve where mustangs used to live, and now it has rich flora and fauna, which is included in the Red Book. It is said that even a couple of centuries ago, the barchans of Dzharylgach were inhabited by camels.

The island's name comes from the Turkic "burnt trees," In Greek sources, Dzharylgach is known as the "island of Achilles."

The island's highlight is the lighthouse, which was designed and built in 1902 by a pupil of the famous architect Eiffel.

This place popular with tourists is the freshwater spring on the seashore.

Recently, the skeleton of a dragon was found on the island. At least that's what social media users claimed, confirming their words with a photo taken in front of the lighthouse. But, as it turns out, this is not the case. And although it's just a lucky prank of Joan Rowling's fans, you must agree that the creature from Newt Scamander's book fits perfectly into Kherson's landscape.

The Legend of Hoverla - the Highest Peak in the Ukrainian Carpathians

Hoverla is the highest mountain peak in Ukraine. Its height is 2061 meters above sea level. It is located in the Carpathian Mountains in the Chornogora Range, on the border of the Ivano-Frankivsk and Zakarpattya regions.

The name "Hoverla" comes from Hungarian "hóvár", which means "snowy mountain". Indeed, the mountaintop is almost always covered with snow - it melts in July, and not always. The mountain became Hoverla because of ... a mistake. Hutsul people originally called it Hovirla, but when Austrian cartographers mapped the area, one of them wrote down Hoverla. That's how the name got around.

There are several legends and tales associated with Ukraine's highest peak. One of them is striking for its romanticism and, at the same time, tragedy. In a nearby village lived a guy, Prut. One day, after his hard labor, he lay down to rest in the shade of the forest. An unbelievably beautiful girl appeared in his dream, but she immediately disappeared as soon as he wanted to stretch out his hand to her. Nathan could not get away from the idea that it was happening. The colorful ribbon Nathan had thoughtlessly left on a tree branch.

He was determined not to let the girl get away with it again. The next time he 'fell asleep' again under the same tree, waited for the girl to arrive, and deftly caught her hand and held it to his heart. She told him her name was Hoverla. They were amazed at this meeting and decided never to part again. The Prut never returned to his village again, and Hoverla spent all her time by her sweetheart's side.

The story might have been happy if the Mountain King, whose daughter Hoverla was, had not found out about it. Her father's anger knew no bounds, and he saw her relationship as a betrayal. He forbade the lovers to see each other. The girl threw herself down from the high cliffs in despair as her heart did not want to be separated from her beloved. The story goes that no sooner had the girl touched the bottom of the abyss than a mighty wind blew up and tore down trees on her way, and after it had died out, a high peak appeared at that place, so high that one could not see its end.

The Prut wandered the mountain paths for a long time trying to find his lost love, and one day he heard a girl singing that touched all the strings of his soul. From then on, he started avoiding other people. A river delimited the peak, and how to name it - the villagers of the surrounding villages did not even hesitate. The new summit was called Hoverla, and the reservoir was named the Prut. People were sure that the story of tragic love would never be forgotten in this way.

It should be said that legends and tales of the Carpathian mountains often become a subject of inspiration for artists. For example, the Carpathian Mountains inspired the novella "The Shadows of Forgotten Ancestors," later filmed. The story of Marichka and Ivan is a bit like a classic love story where the lovers cannot be together because of the original enmity of their families. The presence of other characters - molfars, perelesniks, mawkas, and other evil spirits - adds to the authenticity of the Hutsul Romeo and Juliet story.

Extreme Tourism to the Chornobyl Exclusion Zone

The Chornobyl zone is becoming the most popular destination for foreign tourists visiting Ukraine. Several new tourist sites have been added to the 'traditional pilgrimage sites', the Chornobyl NPP (Nuclear Power Plant) and Pripyat city. The government and territorial communities bordering the Zone say as much as possible about promoting official Chornobyl tourism. As for illegal 'stalker' tourists, the authorities are trying to tighten security in the Exclusion Zone. Meanwhile, radiation monitoring shows radiation levels have dropped precipitously since the accident. So there is no danger to tourists on official trails.

Exclusion Zone guides and tour operators working there claim that visitors are most interested in the abandoned nuclear workers' town of Pripyat, the industrial site of Chornobyl NPP (from where, until recently, one could see the sarcophagus of the fourth unit, but now new safe confinement rises above it) and the former Soviet secret places. Then there are the former Soviet secret facilities on this site and the nature of Ukrainian Polesye, which has fully recovered after three decades of human absence.

The most enigmatic structure in the Exclusion Zone, which has only recently been revealed to tourists and the media, is a Cold War artifact between the USSR and the West - the Duga radar station and the Soviet-era Chornobyl-2 security camp located next to it. A row of metal masts 150 meters high with wires strung between them was planned for use in Soviet times as "over-the-horizon tracking" (detecting ballistic missile launches on other continents) and jamming radio signals in Europe. The construction operated only in test mode before the Chornobyl accident, but it still created interference over Europe, including radio communications and air traffic. For the characteristic rhythmic tapping in the air generated by "The Arc", Western experts called the structure a "communist woodpecker".

During Soviet times, Pripyat, a city of nuclear workers, was considered one of the most modern in Ukraine. But since April 28, 1986, no one has lived here. People were evacuated in a hurry. In an attempt to expedite the process, residents were asked not to take many things and were persuaded that the evacuation was temporary. Therefore, many flats were left with furniture, Soviet-style household appliances, sanitary equipment, and some personal belongings. The houses are gradually deteriorating, so tourists are strongly advised not to visit them.

Meanwhile, the Exclusion Zone administration is considering repairing several houses in Pripyat, restoring the homes to the condition of the day of the accident in 1986, and showing them to tourists.

The unique attraction for visitors is the amusement park: the Ferris wheel, electric cars, and swings. The rides were scheduled to be inaugurated on May 1, 1986. But because of an accident, the children never rode them; just as spooky as the café buildings, overgrown with moss and young trees, the dilapidated department store, and the school classrooms, with their desks rotten with dampness.

Other sights include monumental reliefs on the walls of houses and, next door, more recent, post-abandonment graffiti by international students.

Also striking is the now-empty city swimming pool, which was still in use sometime after the accident: liquidators would swim here after their shifts. Nearby is the tallest 16-story building in the city with a faded Soviet coat of arms on the roof. The city stadium is overgrown with a young forest.

The pier on the Pripyat River was the most radioactive area in town, and until recently it was dangerous even for short stays. But now, the Zone's administration and travel agencies are testing a water tourist route that will link Kyiv and the forgotten city of nuclear workers.

People in Pripyat will never live: radioactive transuranic elements, which contaminate the area near the Chornobyl nuclear power plant, have a half-life of up to 24,000 years, the Ukrainian Environment Ministry says. But in the town of Chornobyl and small villages on the periphery of the Zone, radiation levels are close to those in Kyiv. And that has made it possible for self-settlers to settle there: locals who returned home soon after the accident and lived off their pensions and from their vegetable gardens. They number more than 100 here. Most of them welcome unexpected visitors - when they are visited by tourists, zone workers, or representatives of official delegations.

In Chornobyl, where staff from the Exclusion Zone live and work rotationally, you can see a museum of everyday life in Ukrainian Polesye with thousands of antique things and clothes. And there is another open-air museum featuring examples of machinery that eliminated the accident at unit 4 of the Chornobyl nuclear power plant.

ChNPP curiosities

The scenery of the provisional sarcophagus of the fourth unit of the Chornobyl nuclear power plant has become an obligatory site for excursions. Its silhouette has become an internationally recognizable symbol of the nuclear disaster. But since November 2016, tourists will never see it again: the coffin is covered by new, safe confinement - a sealed metal arch of impressive size, which is believed to be the largest movable surface structure in the world.

The arch has a span of 257 meters, a length of 150 meters, and a height of 108 meters. The containment was built by the experts of the French company Novarka and Ukrainian specialists at a distance from the coffin to avoid irradiation of the personnel. It was then pushed onto the ruined reactor using a system of heavy jacks. In the next hundred years (just for so long as new protective construction is designed), tourists will be photographed against its background. However, next to the observation deck, one can show a relatively accurate model of the destroyed reactor in a cross-section - with internal organs unfolded by the explosion.

Walking around the Chornobyl NPP is forbidden, and in some places, the bus takes visitors at high speed: the dosimeter starts beeping dangerously. Near the western wall of the confinement is the most extensive radiation. In this direction, the radioactive cloud moved immediately after the explosion. However, measurements show that since the protective arch on the reactor sarcophagus was built, radiation levels at the Chornobyl site have decreased many times over: the protective metal arch reduces radiation from Unit 4.

Next to the main entrance to the Chornobyl nuclear power plant is a railway bridge over the cooling pond. When visitors have time - they are encouraged to throw pieces of bread in there and watch. At first, smaller fish come up from the depths to feed. Then a predatory black shadow pushes them away: it is the legendary Chornobyl catfish. The fish can swallow up to half of the bread thrown by tourists or station workers at a time. The fish are a luxury: it is strictly forbidden to fish in the pond because of the super-high radioactive contamination of the water and silt.

Chornobyl nature: human-friendly but vulnerable

Birds of prey nest on balconies like rocks, and bobcats and wild boars use lower-floor flats as natural caves. The former city stadium has become a dense young forest where moose, deer, and roe deer find shelter. This is what the ecosystem formed in Pripyat after the resettlement looks like. Biologists say this is a unique natural community for Polesie, more typical for rocky mountain massifs.

Wild animals of the Exclusion Zone are often not afraid of humans. Thus, many workers of the Zone say that they have seen wolves in winter, which, having noticed a man, did not run away and stayed in sight.

The nature of the Chornobyl zone attracts both scientists and tourists: it is now the most uninhabited and overgrown forested area in Europe. In the early twentieth century, most of the forests around the city of Chornobyl were clear-cut and then reforested with pine. Moreover, before the Chornobyl tragedy, about a hundred thousand people lived in what is now the Zone, statistics show. But for 31 years now, much of the Zone has remained uninhabited.

Chornobyl tourism: from "stalkers" to wealthy foreigners

Stories (with photos and videos) of illegal 'stalker' travelers infiltrating the Exclusion Zone to see the most interesting sites have been appearing on the web since the 1990s.

But times have changed. There is a growing flow of official tourists who can see the wilderness of the Zone and get some essential comfort. A hostel has been opened in the Zone for participants in multi-day tours, media, and scientists: the rooms in Chornobyl's newest home are simple but warm, cozy, and have everything they need.

Khortytsia Island - the Cradle of Zaporizhian Sich

If you want to see Ukraine as it was at the time of the Cossacks - the island of

Khortytsia, located in the glorious Zaporizhzhia, is waiting for you. There are many monuments of antiquity, culture, and architecture, and the historical legacy of the island is due to its location and natural wealth.

Historical background

The first mention of Khortytsia appeared in historical documents in the 10th century, even though people lived there in the Paleolithic and Mesolithic eras. And in the 9th century, there was a road from the Varangians to the Greeks crossing the Dnieper River. And on the island, travelers had the opportunity to rest and gain strength.

Cossack settlements began to appear on the island of Malaya Khortitsa in 1556. Their founder was the famous hetman Dmitry Vishnevetsky - Baida. The settlement was surrounded by paling, there was enough space in Cossack tents for all the residents, and the church of the Holy Protection was erected in the middle of it. This period was the most remarkable in the history of Khortytsia. Its territory was visited by French cartographer Beauplan, who created a map of Ukraine at that time.

After Russian Empress Catherine liquidated the Sich, Prince Grigory Potemkin took over the island. Later, German Mennonites lived there and grew timber to sell. In 1927 the powerful Dnieper hydroelectric power station was built near Khortytsya. During the war in 1941, the NKVD decided to blow up the station to stop the German attack. Thousands of lives were sacrificed not only by the Germans but also by Red Army soldiers and ordinary citizens from surrounding villages.

Sights of the island

Today Khortytsia is known not only in Ukraine but also around the world. Included in the seven wonders of Ukraine, it attracts thousands of tourists every year. They come here to feel the spirit of the Cossacks, to see with their own eyes how our ancestors lived and what they were proud of.

The island's length is 12.5 km, the average width is 2.5 km, and its total area is 23.59 km2. Historians have found a gigantic so-called black stone covered in bizarre inscriptions in the southern part. The largest of these weighs as much as 600 kg.

There are also the oldest oaks in Ukraine. And although most of the giant trees were cut down in the last century, you can still see a tree over 300 years old.

What can you do on the island? Indeed wander the forest paths, breathe in the Dnieper air and see exciting finds, such as an ancient sword from the 10th century. You can also rent a bike or sail on the Dnieper River around Khortytsia Island. Those who love extreme sports are invited to take part in Cossack rides and participate in battle re-enactments.

While traveling around the island, you must visit the following places.

* Historical and cultural complex "Zaporizhian Sich" - here are reconstructed residential and farm buildings, churches, huts, cannon stans, and many other exciting places. Here you can experience the atmosphere of the glorious Cossacks.

* Folklore and Ethnographic Horse Theatre "Zaporizhian Cossacks" - located in the south of the island, the theatre puts on remarkable performances for those who visit. While watching it, everyone feels like they are directly participating in the action.

- Museum of Zaporozhian Cossacks - its exhibits include everything the Cossacks used to use - money, household items, and much more. There is even the sword of Svyatoslav, the pride of the museum.

- Memorial-tourist complex "Scythian Stan" - here you can see ancient burial mounds, most of which were robbed during the Soviet era and plowed up for agricultural land.

Those who want to stay at Khortytsia for a few more days will find hotels, recreation centers, and tourist centers. If you wish, you can also stay in tents at specially allocated places.

Kyiv Pechersk Lavra - Ukrainian Jerusalem

Kyiv is home to one of the oldest Orthodox sanctuaries, a unique monastic complex - Kyiv Pechersk Lavra. It is located on the steep hills of the right bank of the Dnieper River and is majestically crowned with golden domes.

Speaking of history

It was founded as a monastery as early as the 11th century, and over nine centuries, it was continuously altered and rebuilt. In Greek, the name Lavra indicates that it was a mighty and considerable monastery at that time, and the word Pecherska indicates that it was in the caves where the first monks lived. They were gradually joined by other hermits, who dug new cells and built underground churches.

By this time, the shrine was far from Kyiv, the number of monks increased steadily, and soon the first above-ground church of the Assumption of the Blessed Virgin Mary was built. And later, prince Izyaslav Yaroslavovich gave the whole mountain, under which were the caves, as a monastery called Pechersk monastery.

The shrine quickly grew, gradually gaining fame as a cultural center of Kievan Rus. Here the church literature was published, the icon-painting school worked, and perhaps the famous Tale of Igor's Campaign was created. The monastery also became a kind of academy for Orthodox hierarchies.

For many centuries, Lavra suffered raids and wars and was destroyed several times, but each time it was restored again and again. Polovtsians,

Turks, and Tatars plundered it, and a massive fire almost destroyed the wealthiest library of those times and many valuable documents.

In soviet times there was an open museum compound in Lavra. The Ukrainian State Historical Library, which is still located there, was placed there. There is also a Museum of Books, the Museum of Historical Treasures, and other exhibitions. Unfortunately, during World War II, the Cathedral of the Assumption was destroyed, and the monastery's treasures were looted. Nevertheless, the specialists managed to restore much of it by the anniversary of the millennium of Baptism of Russia.

Lavra life today

Nowadays, the complex occupies about 30 hectares. It was entered in the list of the historical and cultural heritage of UNESCO in Ukraine Kievo-Pecherskaya Lavra is noted as a place of honor among the seven wonders of Ukraine. It can be safely called a kind of Ukrainian Jerusalem because millions of pilgrims come to this worship place worldwide.

It is also attractive to tourists. Its principal value is the relics of reverend fathers and noble believers that have been kept in underground caves for hundreds of years. Moreover, there are 144 buildings, 122 of which have historical and cultural value.

Traveling around the Lavra, it is worth seeing:

* Trinity Church of 1108, one of the oldest in the area;

- Holy Gate under which, according to legend, you'll be absolved of half your sins;

* Baroque Cathedral of the Assumption, which houses the prominent relics of the Lavra;

* Great Lavra Bell Tower, 96 m high, built by architect Schedel;

* The cells of the cathedral elders where the monks spent their lives praying for people;

- the labyrinths of the Near and Far Caves, whose total length exceeds 500 meters;

* the underground churches of the Nativity, the Annunciation of the Blessed Virgin Mary, and others.

By the way, the holy relics can be seen in the underground cells of the monks. There are also myrrh heads there, which have healing properties and help all who come here in faith. They say that during the Soviet regime, when only museums were here, they were not myrrh-stained and only resumed when the monastery returned to the Lavra.

Synevyr - the Heart and Soul of the Carpathians

Lake Synevyr is one of the most beautiful and mysterious places in Ukraine. It is located near the village Synevirskaya Polyana, Mezhigorie district, Zakarpattya region. Another name is Sea-Eye. If you look at it from above, you can see the following picture: an extensive reservoir surrounded by mighty trees from all sides with a small island in the middle that resembles a pupil. Every year it attracts a lot of tourists not only from Ukraine but also from all over the world.

History of formation

About 10 thousand years ago, there was an earthquake, which caused a powerful landslide. The rocks stood in the way of the stream, and a dam was formed. The dam created a basin filled with the waters of three creeks.

Interesting facts about Synevyr

- The depth of the lake reaches 24 meters in some places. The average depth is 8-10 m.

-The lake is the home of the brown trout, a fish that lives only in crystal clear water. Indeed, if you look at the surface, you can see the bottom.

- The water is cold even in summer due to the location and depth. The average temperature is 10-19 degrees, but the water gets warm to only 1-2 meters. Swimming in the lake is prohibited.

- Synevyr is the largest and the deepest alpine lake in the Carpathians. There are 32 of them in total.

- The lake is ranked among the top seven natural wonders of Ukraine.

- Not far from the lake, there is a unique and the only place in the country - the Brown Bear Rehabilitation Centre. Here they take care of the animals which have lived in an inappropriate environment or have been abused.

- Sea-Eye is located in a nature reserve, where you can see animals and plants that are listed in the Red Book. If you are lucky, you may come across mountain roe deer, deer, badger, ermine, and other animals. Littering, making a fire, setting up tents, hunting animals, or destroying plants is strictly forbidden.

- A mahogany sculpture of two lovers, Sina and Viru, has been erected near the lake.

-The lake is located in the Synevyr National Park.

- When heading here, be sure to bring more bread with you. There are so many trout in the lake's crystal clear waters, and they behave so brazenly that they will snatch bread crumbs from your hands.

- The lake is a popular location not only for amateur videos but also for full-blown movies. It is so alluring with its mystique that a horror film of the same name was made about it, released in 2013. The Synevyr was also mentioned in such films as The Tragedy of Carpathian Ukraine, Chervona Ruta, and Ursus. And in 2018, the Ukrainian-French film The Last Step, starring Jean Renault, was filmed here.

- The lake covers an area of about 5 hectares.
- It is situated at an altitude of 989 meters above sea level.
- The approximate age of the lake is 10 thousand years.
- Pure mountain air near the Sea-Eye has healing qualities, and it is particularly recommended to visit this place for people with lung diseases.

Legend of the lake

There are many interesting legends about the lake. The most popular tells of the tragic love affair between the daughter of a rich man named Sinja and a simple shepherd named Vir. The father became enraged that his only daughter had fallen in love with a simple boy and ordered his men to drop a stone block on him. This upset Xin so much that she cried a whole lake of tears, later named Synevyr.

Synevyr is one of the most popular tourist destinations. It attracts all kinds of people: some come here for the spectacular photos, some to find peace and tranquillity, some to enjoy the fresh pine air and nature, and others to enjoy the pleasant hiking trails and the local traditions. It is undoubtedly an incredible place that every tourist should visit at least once.

Lake Lemuria - the Dead Sea in Ukraine

If you have no opportunity to go to the Dead Sea in the Middle East, do not despair. In Ukraine, there is a kind of analog of this reservoir - Lemurian lake, which has another name - Pink. However, locals call it just a pit because of the exciting history of the lake's origin.

In the late 60s of the last century, near the village of Grigorivka, in the Kherson region, a Soviet military aircraft crashed. It hit the ground with such force that a large crater was formed. After the military collected and removed the wreckage, the pit slowly began to fill up with water from an underground spring. As it turned out, the water had curative properties and pleasant pink color. The explanation is somewhat prosaic - algae blooming makes this effect possible. But the result is impenetrable to those who see it for the first time.

Some researchers claim the lake to be the remnants of the prehistoric Lemurian Sea. Whether it's true or not, this place could be used as a backdrop for making sci-fi movies. Periodically, a slight recession in the water reveals a truly Martian landscape, with crusty pink plains where the blue sky reflects and old trees overgrown with salt crystals.

Unique qualities of the lake

According to some reports, the salt concentration in the water reaches 270-300 grams per liter. In comparison, in the Dead Sea, it is only slightly more - 350 grams. So, if you want to read the newspaper while lying on the pink water surface, you can certainly do it.

Researchers working in the area for seven years have found a wealth of minerals, acids, nitrogenous substances, carbohydrates, sodium iodide, magnesium and potassium chloride salts, and magnesium bromide in the water. Interacting with the muds of Sivash, in whose bay the lake is located, dramatically enhances its healing properties. That is why this place is now considered a health resort, which is confirmed by the Institute of Medical Rehabilitation of the Ministry of Health of Ukraine.

It should be noted that studies have also revealed the fact that the mud at the lake is not of natural origin. This is the only case in the history of Earth when man has interfered with nature and created something like a bomb. The mud is believed to be a powerful immune booster, and there are many known cases of favorable results in treating many diseases. People come here to improve their condition in case of cystitis, tonsillitis, psoriasis, radiculitis, neurosis, vegetovascular dystonia, and other diseases.

By the way, the locals authoritatively assert that the lake's pink water also serves as a specific "anti-cop". They believe bathing in the reservoir in a state of intoxication contributes to sobering up immediately. Scientists have found an explanation for this unique phenomenon - brine Sivash, it turns out, has elements that significantly enhance the purifying function of the liver.

The miraculous properties of mud are already well known abroad - to Kherson, tourists come from Europe, and foreign cosmetic firms are seriously interested in exporting healing resources from Ukraine.

Until recently, the village Grigorivka itself, situated only 4 km from the unique lake, was doomed to extinction. But in recent years, it has been actively developing green tourism thanks to the lake. And today, around 40 farmsteads hospitably invite holidaymakers and those who want to improve their health.

The Tunnel of Love - a Jewel of the Rivne Region

Her Majesty the Nature has created many unique masterpieces, many of which can be found on the territory of Ukraine. The Tunnel of Love - this is the name of the Magic Place in the Rivne region, near the town of Klevan. Everyone who has visited it can't hide their sincere admiration. The tunnel can be regarded as a natural botanical phenomenon - created by intertwined branches and shoots of bushes, it overhangs directly above the railway track, enchanting and luring you into the distance.

Where did it come from?

The Tunnel of Love has only recently become extremely popular - just a dozen years ago, few people had heard of it. Today, it is the most romantic place in Ukraine, so newlyweds, lovers, or friends come here to enjoy the view.

And it was formed almost by accident. During Soviet times, this part of the railway was directed to the military base. For maximum concealment of train traffic, it was decided to plant trees on both sides of the track. After a while, the railway was no longer needed, the trees were no longer trimmed, and they gradually covered all possible space with an intricate tangle of branches and leaves.

But one small train does run there. Thanks to it, the tunnel has acquired such a perfect shape. The locomotive breaks branches on the track and forms a picturesque arch. The train itself blends so seamlessly into the overall atmosphere that few tourists turn down the chance to take a beautiful photo.

The Tunnel of Love is magical at any time of year. In summer, it resembles a fairy-tale green cave inhabited by elves. In autumn, there's a veritable riot of colors-golden, hot yellow, reddish-brown, orange-green... In winter, the tunnel is not surpassed either - the white clothes of trees give it majesty and mystery.

Interesting facts and legends

Locals say that the souls of a couple in love roam here, once forbidden to get married by their parents. The girl threw herself into a nearby swamp because of grief, and her boyfriend searched for her for a long time, so she disappeared without a trace. Now their pure souls help other lovers, and so everyone who comes here believes:

* walking in this area during a wedding will contribute to a happy married life in the future;

* if a couple makes a mutual wish under the archway, it will come true;

* visiting the tunnel is a romantic means of establishing marital relations.

It should be noted that in 2014, Japanese director Akioshi Imazaki filmed a romantic film here, Klevan. Tunnel of Love", after which the area became a pilgrimage destination for tourists from Japan. There are also many commercials filmed in Klevan, including one by the Japanese company Fujifilm.

Celebrities from Ukraine

Anna Yaroslavna - Queen of France

K ievan Rus was a powerful state whose heyday was at the end of the 10th and 11th centuries. One of the rulers who brought the country to this peak was Yaroslav the Wise. During his reign Christianity got spread and strengthened, chronicles were created, icon writing developed, schools and libraries were opened, and many books were translated into Church Slavonic.

At this time of the rise, in 1032, perhaps the ruler's most famous daughter, Anna Yaroslavna, was born. Together with her brothers and sisters, the princess received a good education. She studied mathematics, grammar, and knowledge of history and mastered the Greek and Latin languages. Cultural evenings with poets, jesters, and musicians were held in the prince's chambers. Anna's magical beauty and kind heart were the talks of the town throughout Europe.

When her daughter grew up, the Grand Duke began to choose a worthy match for her. Yaroslav was a wise politician and wanted to strengthen foreign political connections through marriages between his children and European monarchs. The prince hesitated for a long time, but the French King Henry, with his persistence, won his consent to marry Anna.

Anna Yaroslavna, like every girl, dreamed of a magic prince and a fairy-tale land where they would live and rule. But unfortunately, her husband was not a young king of France, whose first wife died, and his political situation was relatively unstable. The marriage to the Ukrainian princess was to strengthen his position and support the mighty state.

After traveling more than two thousand kilometers in two months, almost all over Eastern Europe, and learning the French language, Anne arrived in the small town of Senlis. After meeting her fiancé for the first time, the princess's hopes and dreams crumbled like a house of cards. Heinrich was a fifty-year-old, heavy, and sullen man. But, despite this, the wedding and coronation of Anne of Rheims took place in the cathedral of Rheims on May 19, 1051. The girl brought her valuable gifts, including books inlaid with precious stones. But the King did not appreciate her efforts because the courtiers did not know letters and could not read. In France in XI century, only clergymen were educated. Moreover, Paris in 1051 had no sewerage system; it was dirty and smelly. Locals threw rubbish from windows into the street, did not wash because they considered it a mortal sin, and ate with their hands.

What a barbaric country you have sent me to; here, the dwellings are bleak, the churches ugly, and the manners horrible... You said the French were clever people who don't even know a letter. I showed the book to the King. He grimaced and said, "I'm not a priest to read so much. We don't have a king in Europe who can't read."

Every day she went to sleep with the thought that tomorrow she would flee from that grim and dirty country, but every morning she woke up and had to fulfill the role assigned to her by her father and fate.

So the Queen decided to remedy the situation and started teaching literacy to the King and courtiers, making them use pitchforks. The wisdom and diplomatic skills taught to her at home enabled Anne to win the affections not only of the French but even of Pope Nicholas II.

The birth of an heir helped further cement her position in foreign lands. Then, in 1053, Philip I came of age in the royal family. Anne subsequently bore Henry two more sons, one of whom, Robert, died in his teens, and the other, Hugo, became one of the leaders of the Crusades.

Anna Yaroslavna devoted herself entirely to the education of her children. She taught them literacy, mathematics, foreign languages, singing, and drawing.

Henry was a rather clever ruler, and his wife helped him in state affairs. Later, Anne's signature began to appear next to the King's on documents. Her grasp of public affairs immensely helped when Henry Carpeting died suddenly of a heart attack in 1060.

As a widow, Anne did not become regent to the infant prince because the law said only the nearest male relative could do so. That honor fell to the Earl of Baldwin of Flanders, but Anne stayed close to her son Philip and signed some documents with him.

All went quietly until love came into the life of the thirty-year-old Queen. A sympathy that began while the King was still alive grew into a great love. Raoul VI, Count of Valois, an opponent of Henry I and had been called the 'devil', was madly in love with the beauty of Kyiv. So despite his marriage in 1062, the Earl kidnaps Anne and secretly marries her.

This caused a great scandal. The Earl's lawful wife, Eleonora, could not bear the disgrace and wrote a letter to the Pope. As Pope Nicholas II had corresponded with the Queen of France, he demanded that Anne break the shameful alliance and return to Paris and excommunicated Raoul VI. But Anne ignored this letter and, with Count Valois, happily lived ten years in the small town of Senlis. In this town, she built the monastery of St Vincent in 1065.

In 1066, at the age of fourteen, Philip I was crowned. Subsequently, he married Bertha of Fraysinchen and France received a new queen. Anne helped her son in every way she could, and despite her scandal and absence, she had considerable weight in public affairs management. Her signature continued to feature prominently in documents. So when her beloved count died in 1074, she was able to return to Paris. Her signature was last recorded on the papers of 1075. Historians believe that it was in this year that Anna of Kyiv died.

Interesting Facts

In Kyiv, Anna was engaged in rewriting books for the library.

French monarchs had long sworn allegiance to France on the Gospel of Reims, which Anne brought during the coronation, without knowing what language the book was written in.

For her literacy, her detractors often called her a witch.

She was the only woman to correspond with Pope Nicholas II.

Under the first monument to the Queen in the town of Senlis, the inscription reads 'Anne of Rus, Queen of France'. In September 1996, the inscription was changed to "Anne of Kyiv, Queen of France".

Few people know, but Anne and Henry had sons and a daughter called Edigne. In 1074 her elder brother and King Philip I decided to marry her. The girl was against it and fled from Paris. She found refuge in the Bavarian town of Pugh. There she lived all her life, taught children, and cured the sick. For these good deeds, in 1600, the Catholic Church proclaimed her Blessed One. Holy relics of the granddaughter of Yaroslav the Wise can be found in the chapel church in Puch, 30 km from Munich. People still come to her, asking for help and strength to fight illnesses.

Roksolana - Ukrainian at the Head of the Ottoman Empire

Legendary Roksolana is one of the most famous and mysterious women of late medieval Ukrainian history. Her journey from an unhappy captive to one of the world's most powerful rulers surprises not only with its drama but also with its dizzying twists and turns, worthy of an adventure novel.

Roksolana was the first and only woman in the history of the Ottoman Empire to receive an official title. Roksolana was considered Haseki sultaness, which meant she was co-ruler of the Sublime Porte, and Sultan Suleiman shared his power with her.

European ambassadors were at a loss for words when Roksolana sat on the throne next to her husband with an open face. She did not resemble a submissive Asian woman but an ancient Egyptian Cleopatra.

Roksolana's name is linked to many changes in the Turkish capital. The sultaness tried her best to be engaged in education and gave much time to charity. The Avret Bazar district of Istanbul, where Roksolana built a mosque, a hospital, and an orphanage for the poor, is now named after her. Turks are convinced that many architectural monuments in Istanbul are directly linked to Roksolana-Hurrem. They hold the woman's name in high esteem, and her tomb is considered one of the country's national treasures.

While Roksolana was in power in the Ottoman Empire, she did everything to prevent the Crimean Tatars from plundering her homeland, Ukraine.

Anastasia Lisovska was the daughter of a priest from the western Ukrainian town of Rohatyn. Legend has it that in 1522 on her wedding day, the young Anastasia was abducted by the Tatars and taken to a slave market in Cafe, then on to Istanbul. There the vizier of Sultan Suleiman I purchased her for his master.

The Sultan's harem gave her a new name, Roksolana ("Roksolans" were the Sarmatians whom the Turks thought to be the ancestors of the Slavs). Charming Anastasia was also nicknamed Hürrem (the laughing one). Roksolana's beauty has been given many nice words, though eyewitnesses from Rogatine described her as pretty rather than beautiful. The Venetian Navaggero also wrote that Roksolana was "young but not beautiful, though she looked charming". Unlike many other beauties, she was pretty educated; she was literate and later learned several languages (Turkish, Arabic, and Persian). Roksolana asked for the right to visit the Sultan's library from the start and wasted no time in constant self-education. She did not hesitate to convert to Islam so that her children could claim the throne of the Ottoman Empire.

The simple concubine succeeded in becoming the Sultan's favorite wife. Their wedding took place in 1534, and it was an unprecedented occasion: the Sultan married a woman from the harem. Suleiman and Roksolana were a loving couple; they could talk about politics and art for hours, often communicating in verse. Their feelings were mutual and very sincere, as evidenced by the couple's correspondence lines. My Sultan," Roksolana wrote, "what a boundless and searing pain of parting. Save me, wretched one, and do not delay with your beautiful letters. May my soul receive at least a drop of joy from your messages. When they are read to us, your servant and son Mehmed and your slave and daughter Migrima weep, yearning for you. Their tears drive me mad." "My dear goddess, my wondrous beauty," he replied, "mistress of my heart, my brightest month, my most profound desires companion, my only one, you are dearer to me than all the beauties of the world!

The Sultan was allowed much; she even appeared in public with an open face, which in no way damaged her reputation as an exemplary Muslim. The couple had three sons and a daughter.

The ambitious Roksolana made her wildest dreams come true and ensured that her son Selim would inherit the throne. Standing in her way was Sultan's eldest son by his first wife, the beautiful Circassian Gulbeher. His father's favorite, Mustafa, was also very popular with the people. Using this fact to arouse Suleyman's fears and jealousy, Roksolana assured him that her son, together with Vizier Rustem Pasha, was allegedly plotting a state plot.

After severe torture, the vizier was executed. In the meantime, he was Roksolana's son-in-law: she married him to her young daughter, with whose help she collected the necessary information. Mustafa was soon treacherously murdered: he was strangled by order and even in the presence of his father. The heir to the throne's mother went mad and shortly died. After this, Roksolana's position in court and her son's future was no longer threatened.

Roksolana was the wife of Suleiman the Pompous for forty years. She died of her own accord, leaving her husband a widower. She did not get to see her son ascend the throne, becoming Sultan Selim II. After his father's death, he ruled for eight years from 1566 to 1574, though he was more famous for his drunkenness than his statesmanship.

Undoubtedly, Roksolana was helped by her beauty, cunning, cruelty, and uncommon intelligence. She was in personal correspondence with rulers of neighboring states (Poland, Venice, Persia), knew the Koran to perfection, and was engaged in art.

She wielded real influence over the politics of the country. Roksolana is credited with the fact that raids on Ukrainian lands became less active thanks to her Tatar.

Ukrainian Yuriy Budyak Saved Winston Churchill

Fate brought the legendary British Prime Minister Winston Churchill and the little-known Ukrainian writer Yurii Budyak together in South Africa during the Boer War. The war was triggered by discovering gold and diamond deposits, which the British decided to appropriate for themselves. There was outrage at the invasion, and volunteers from all over the world came to help the Africans. Ukrainians were among them.

On October 11, 1899, the Second Boer War broke out. The British wanted to take control of the gold and diamond deposits in the independent republics of Orange and Transvaal. But the beleaguered Dutch colonizer-founders of the young African republics did not want to put up with this geopolitical situation. Nor did the young Poltava-born poet Yuriy Budyak wish to put up with this state of affairs. The maverick decided to stand up for Africa and went to fight on the faraway Black Continent.

Yuriy Budyak, in his 20s, had time to visit both the Crimea and the Caucasus. He was a sailor, a longshoreman, and even wrote articles for newspapers. The adventurous young man, having heard about the audacity of the British, set off for the "black" continent. At first, he was a private and, having mastered the language, took charge of an entire squadron. His fighters operated mostly underground and laid traps for the British.

Yuri Budyak can be safely called the Ukrainian Indiana Jones. Like the hero of adventure films, he wandered the world, fought against injustice, and cut off the heads of those who caused this injustice.

Arriving in Africa, Yuri Budyak first fights as a common soldier and heads a guerrilla group of Boer rebels. The point is that the Dutch refuse to attack the enemy with large military formations. When the Boers vastly outnumbered the British forces, and the soldiers from Albion were better armed than the guns and revolvers of the "Orange", guerrilla warfare was the best way to fight.

The Boers decided to use the famous Spanish tactic "Guerilla". Its essence is that small, mobile insurgent units strike the enemy by surprise, attacking convoys, encircling backward enemy soldiers, blowing up railway tracks, destroying telegraph lines, intercepting enemy scouts, raid hornets' swarms on military trains, cut enemy troops off from food-stores, keep them in constant tension, starve soldiers and horses and by the aggregate of all these actions inflict heavy losses on enemy armies, the ranks of which thinned day by day.

In November 1899, a detachment attacked an armored train carrying soldiers. Most were immediately shot, and the rest were taken prisoner. One young man stood out among the soldiers. He had no weapons, only a notebook and his press I.D. for The Morning Post.

And one British correspondent was very lucky in this respect. When he was captured by the Boers and dark clouds of death hung over his life, and the hot muzzle of a gun was already looking in his direction, Yuri Budyak activated the "humanity" mode. He prevented fellow soldiers from finishing off a young man with a pencil and a notebook in his pocket. It turned out that that "young and green" reporter was Winston Churchill - the future British Prime Minister. He rode with British soldiers on an armored train, and the Poltava "Indiana Jones" partisans decorated the track with several kilos of dynamite, making it detonate at the right moment. Bang! The train derails, and the soldiers are killed. Those who survived are taken prisoner.

Yuri Budyak did not rush to take the prisoner to headquarters. And this decision already saved Poltava journalist's life the next day. The British troops received reinforcements and surrounded the Boer rebel bombers. Now death was breathing down Yuri's neck. But Mr. Churchill is a polite paparazzi. He tells his fellow villagers that the Boer cape saved him, and they let the young man go home.

That day he was the only one to be spared his life on Budyak's orders. The next day, the British defeated the Boer squad. And now it was Churchill's turn to thank his savior: instead of a prison camp, Budyak ended up in England, in Lord Churchill's family castle. The future politician's family was generous with the reward. Yuri was paid to study at Oxford.

However, the Ukrainian knew too little English, and he wanted to go home. Walking the halls of the world's most prestigious university, Budyak asked for money for a trip to America. He did not get refused either.

His experiences helped Budyak become a journalist and later a children's author back home. Churchill never mentioned the events in South Africa. Yuri Budyak shared his memories only with his closest friends.

Igor Sikorsky - Creator of Helicopters

"Mr. Helicopter" and the "father of helicopter building" is the name given to the creator of the first airplanes and the first American helicopters. Mr. Sikorsky personally, or under his leadership, developed 78 different flying machines. Of these, 72 were built in series, two were taken to the prototype stage, and only four remained on paper.

Igor Sikorsky was born and educated in Kyiv. His father, Ivan Sikorsky -

a well-known psychiatrist, psychologist, pedagogue, and professor of Kyiv Saint Volodymyr University (nowadays named after Taras Shevchenko), was one of the founders of a new line of research in the field of child psychology and psychopathology.

His mother, Maria, played a vital role in his life. She was a highly educated woman. Little Igor loved to listen to his mother's stories about the infinity of the universe, about the beautiful and exciting world. But most of all, the boy's imagination was captured by stories about the 15th-century genius Leonardo da Vinci and his idea to create an "iron bird" - a flying machine, which had to rise into the air under a powerful propeller without any acceleration.

The Sikorski House still stands in the center of Kyiv. Here it is worth remembering that Igor built and tested his first helicopters in the yard of this house. And already, at the age of 19, Sikorsky started to make real planes. At the age of 20, a student of Kyiv Polytechnic Institute, Sikorsky designed and built his first helicopter.

In 1919 Sikorsky from Kyiv emigrated to the USA. Later he set up a cell of former countrymen (1923) involved in aviation. So it was they who paved the way for Sikorski Air Engineering, which became the flagship helicopter technology in the world after World War II.

Igor Sikorski's giant aircraft, the Ilya Muromets (1913), became a world record holder for lifting capacity. Sikorsky also designed the first amphibian aircraft in the USA.

In America, the Ukrainian aircraft designer created 15 types of aircraft and became famous worldwide as the "father of helicopter engineering". Sikorsky's S mark 1941 helicopters were adopted by the US Army.

After World War II, his company Sicorski Air Engineering became the leading helicopter manufacturer abroad.

The last of the helicopters designed personally by Mr. Sikorski in 1954-1955 was the S-58. Its numerous modifications were operated in almost 50 countries worldwide.

Interesting facts

In addition to designing, Sikorsky wrote religious and philosophical books and pamphlets, which experts rank among the most original works of theological thought.

He received more than 80 awards, prizes, and diplomas, including the John Fritz Medal of Honour for scientific and technical achievements in basic and applied sciences.

Sacher Von Masoch - Born and Lived in Ukraine

Although most people associate him with a specific sexual culture and his name suggests his German origins, Sacher von Masoch was born and lived in Ukraine, in the town of Lemberg, now Lviv, which was part of the Austro-Hungarian Empire. There is even a monument to Masoch in the city, which stands by the restaurant with the same name. One can get quite seriously whipped in the back - such as the local "color".

Speaking of the works of Herr Leopold, first of all, it should be noted that the idea of him among modern people who have not read it is somewhat distorted. The term "sado-masochism", ingrained in the public mind, immediately leads one to imagine provocative and naturalistic texts close in spirit to the novels of the Marquis de Sade. Introduced by the German-Austrian psychiatrist Richard von Kraft-Ebing, the terms 'sadism' and 'masochism' describe related phenomena. Still, the writer Sacher-Masoch and de Sade have nothing in common. Masoch's books are pretty harmless and even sentimental, and the sexual deviations in the writer's most famous novel, Venus in Furs, are reflexed by the hero. Written on the wave of dubious success of the novel collection of short stories, "Fatal Women" is intended to develop the theme. Still, fans of BDSM literature will find nothing.

However, the writer's bibliography is not exhausted by 'masochistic' works. Few of his books have been translated into English. The 2009 translation of 'A Snake in Paradise' is almost entirely free of masochistic allusions, except in passing and at will. Instead, the reader is presented with a light and somewhat drawn-out comic novel - nearly a vaudeville. Unpretentious light works constitute the lion's share of Masoch's oeuvre.

Mazoch did indeed earn the love of his compatriots - western Europe learned about the culture of Austro-Hungarian Ukrainians thanks to him. His ethnographic sketches and descriptions of Galician life in his works of fiction. He had a great interest and sympathy for East Slavic culture and the cultures of other peoples who inhabited the region. "Novels of the Rusyn Court", "Galician Tales", and "Jewish Stories" all enriched the culture of Eastern and Western Europe.

A curious fact from modern times. The Zaher-Masoch family gave European culture more than one Herr Leopold. The famous British singer Marinna Faithfull, known for her wild rock youth, collaborates with many notable musicians (of course, with Mick Jagger and The Rolling Stones). Her solo work is a relative of Masoch, who is her great-uncle.

The Famous Klitschko Brothers Have Been Added to The Guinness Book of Records for their Boxing Prowess

Vitali and Wladimir Klitschko have been added to the Guinness Book of Records as the brother champions who combined the most fights.

Together with his brother Wladimir, Vitali began their professional carrier at the age of 25, in 1996, shortly after their Olympic gold in Atlanta 1996.

The first steps on the pro ring the Ukrainians made under the auspices of Hamburg club Universum Box-Promotion.

As a pro, Klitschko had 47 fights, from which he won 45. He won 41 of them before the knockout.

In his last fight on September 8, 2012, in Moscow, Russia, he stopped in the fourth round German of Syrian descent, Manuel Charr. After that, he decided to quit boxing with some hesitation, dedicating himself entirely to political activities. Today, Vitali Klitschko is the mayor of Kiev.

In June 2018, Vitali Klitschko became the first Ukrainian to be inducted into the International Boxing Hall of Fame, located in Canastota Township, New York, USA.

His younger brother Wladimir defeated 23 opponents in 25 world title fights during his career, which is the best record in boxing history among legitimate champions. Still unbeaten is his description of 12 years of total world heavyweight titleholding.

Vladimir has won the title of Ukrainian boxing champion five times. He has held the WBO, IBF, IBO, and WBA world heavyweight and super heavyweight titles during his career.

In August 2017, the younger Klitschko announced the end of his sporting career. At the same time, he expressed his readiness for a new challenge.

Andriy Shevchenko - Golden Ball Winner and Ukraine's Most Famous Footballer

He has already gone down in history as the coach who broke the curse of the group stages of the Ukraine national team at the European championships. He continues to be one of the best Ukrainian footballers in history.

Andriy Shevchenko was born in the village of Dvorkivschyna in the Kyiv region. This village you can hardly find on the map. In time his parents moved to Kyiv, and Shevchenko remained a star in the town. There was even a local FC Andriy Shevchenko team.

At the Dynamo school selection, Shevchenko was overlooked. Only later, in tournaments, he was noticed by the coach Oleksandr Shpakov, who offered the boy to try again. By the way, it was this coach who left Shevchenko in football. After all, his father, Mykola Grygorievich, is a military man. He was against his son's passion for football and wanted Shevchenko junior to receive a decent education.

They came to an agreement man to man - the father, the coach, and Andriy: if there are no bad grades, you can play, but if you fail in your studies, you can forget about football. Shevchenko managed to do everything at school and in sports.

Shevchenko made his debut at Dynamo Kyiv at the age of 18. At first, he played at the right midfielder position rather than forward.

On November 5, 1997, there was a return match in the Champions League, where Dynamo played against the titled Barcelona. In the first leg, the Catalans were defeated in Kyiv 0-3. However, Barcelona failed again at Camp Nou to oppose Lobanovsky's team - 0:4, with Andriy Shevchenko scoring three goals and Serhiy Rebrov scoring the fourth.

In 2003, Shevchenko scored the winning goal in the penalty shoot-out against Juventus from Turin, helping AC Milan win the Champions League.

Andriy dedicated the goal and the victory to the memory of Valeriy Lobanovskiy, who did not live one year to see his talented pupil triumph. Each of the champions is entitled to bring the silver amphora, the Champions League trophy, back home for three days. Arriving in Kyiv with the Champions Trophy, Shevchenko first drove to the Baikove cemetery and his teacher's monument.

Andriy Shevchenko won the Ballon d'Or in 2004. He is the third Ukrainian player named Europe's best footballer, while Oleg Blokhin and Igor Belanov have also claimed the title.

In Hebrew, the word 'Sheva' means the number seven. Israeli fans often say it is destiny, as Shevchenko scored many goals under that number. However, it is worth recalling that Andriy Shevchenko started playing in a T-shirt with the number nine on the back. Under this number, he scored his first Champions League goal - against Bayern (Germany) in 1994.

"Sheva is still Ukraine's all-time leading goalscorer. He has 48 goals under his belt. He has also been the top scorer three times in the Champions League and twice in the Italian league.

Shevchenko has not officially hung up his shoe. He did not announce the end of his career as an active player. There was no farewell match or special press conference.

He first tried out as an assistant to head coach Mykhailo Fomenko, and after his departure, Shevchenko himself took charge of the Ukraine national team. This news was not initially received very well because a good player is not always a good coach. First, one should pass the level of youth teams, clubs, youth national teams, and then the national team.

But the first victory has not been long in coming. Under Andriy Shevchenko, the Ukraine national team finished first in the group in the National League. Then, the sensational exit of Ukraine to Euro 2020, and then a historic victory and the quarterfinal. If Ukraine supporters are grateful to Sweden for getting into the 1/8 finals, they thank only their home nation for this game.

Despite an injury to his back at the 2012 UEFA European Championship, Shevchenko played his best against Sweden. His two goals against Sweden led to a 2-1 win for Ukraine. After nine years again, the Ukrainian team beats Sweden with the same score, but Shevchenko already leads the 'blue-yellows' as a coach. He was the first coach of the Ukrainian team, who took the team to the playoffs and reached the quarterfinals.

The Ukraine national football team debuted at the 2006 FIFA World Cup. In the opening game, Oleh Blokhin's team lost to the Spaniards but reached the 1/8 finals, beating Saudi Arabia and Tunisia. In the 1/8 finals, they beat Switzerland in the penalty shoot-out. Andriy Shevchenko was then captain of the team. It was the only quarterfinal game in which the Ukrainian national team played until 2021.

The Blue-Yellows had already been led to their second quarterfinal by Shevchenko, not as captain but as a coach.

In 2021, the book "Forza Gentile. La mia vita, il mio calcio" (The Silent Power. My life, my football). This is Shevchenko's autobiography, written in collaboration with journalist Alessandro Alciato. It tells some interesting facts about the life of the legendary Ukrainian football player, head coach of the Ukrainian national football team, not only in sports but also in his personal life.

Andriy Shevchenko and Kristen Pazik raise four sons - Jordan, Christian, Alexander, and Ryder Gabriel.

Ukraine's Dmytro Khristych is One of the Most Prolific Ice Hockey Players in NHL History

Ukrainian Dmytro Khristych, for 12 seasons, glorified Ukraine in the NHL, the strongest club hockey league in the world. He played twice in the league

All-Star Game and made over $15 million.

The Ukrainian played in a three-person roster with legendary Canadian Wayne Gretzky in the Los Angeles Kings. In the "Boston Bruins", he twice sued the club. And in Toronto, almost every resident of this Canadian city knew him by sight.

The future champion was born in Kyiv. At 16, he started playing for the Sokol team in the capital, and at 21, he became a World Cup triumphant with the national team of the Soviet Union.

After his meteoric rise to stardom, Khristich headed off to the Atlantic to conquer the NHL, the most prestigious hockey league in the world.

Since 1993, the Ukrainian defended the Washington Capitals and later played for the Los Angeles Kings, Boston Bruins, and Toronto Maple Leafs.

He has been invited to the NHL All-Star Game twice, in 1997 and 1999. He led the independent Ukraine national team to the World Championships three times.

At the Winter Olympics in Salt Lake City, he was part of the blue-yellow team and made it to the top ten national teams of the world.

Dmytro Hrystych is rightfully considered the brightest star of Ukrainian hockey. His record - 811 games in the strongest hockey league on the planet - has not been beaten by any other Ukrainian ever to play in the NHL.

He finished his hockey career in 2004. But, as it turned out, he could not live without a stick in his hands.

In 2009, the former hockey player took 9th place in the Ukrainian Golf Cup, adding to his long list of regalia the position of Vice President of the Ukrainian Golf Federation.

Hollywood Actress Mila Jovovich is Ukrainian

Mila Jovovich is often called the embodiment of the American dream. But not many people know that the star of world cinema is Ukrainian and from Kyiv.

The last name Mila is not correctly read Jovovich, but Yo-vo-vitch. Her father's surname is Bogdan Yo-vo-vitch.

Mila's biography began as the story of an ordinary girl. And perhaps, her life would have turned out very differently if her mother hadn't decided to take her to the United States.

Mila's father was a pediatrician. On the other hand, her mother's biography tells the story of what we might have seen in typical Soviet films. Galina Loginova starred in films such as Shadows Fade at Noon and Much Ado About Nothing.

After marriage, Galina and Bogdan lived in Dnepropetrovsk. Mila went to kindergarten, like all children her age. Then came 1979. Her parents decided to emigrate to the United States of America. Of course, they took Mila with them. At first, though, their family lived in London, then in Sacramento, but eventually, they came to Los Angeles, where they stayed forever.

In America, the Yo-vo-vitch family began to be called Jovovich, and Mila began to write her name with two "l "s. Living in a foreign country was very difficult at first. Galina and Bogdan, people with higher education, worked as ordinary servants in the family of director de Palma. Mila was still too young to work, and she went to school.

In the early eighties, the cold war made itself felt again. All her classmates knew that Mila was from the Soviet Union. For this, the girl was treated with distrust. But this only strengthened the girl's pride in her roots.

"I succeeded because of the tremendous willpower I owe my origins," Jovovich claims in interviews.

Mila's mother knew she would never be able to be a full-fledged actress in America, but her daughter had every chance. Especially since Mila - is a brilliant and talented girl. That's why her mother decided to do everything she could so that her daughter could succeed. She worked hard to pay for Mila's music, dance, and acting classes.

But, no matter how hard it was for Galina, her hard work soon began to pay off. At the age of eleven, Mila appeared on the cover of the Italian magazine Lei. And soon, the girl was already invited to a photo shoot in "Mademoiselle" magazine. Incidentally, at the time, there was some confusion and excitement about the fact that the model was underage.

There was a buzz around Milla, and, as you know, black PR promotes and promotes the best. So while the fact that Mila is involved in photo shoots was discussed on American television, she was shot for dozens of different magazines. The Jovovich family finally began to have some decent money, and it's all thanks to Mila.

But still, we should never forget about the actress's mother. She constantly helped her daughter, trying to do everything to ensure she did not ruin her talent and achieve maximum results. But Mila was a teenager, so she often did not listen to her mother. Especially since she had her own money, the fifteen-year-old girl seemed to be already independent and could do anything she saw fit. At that age, she and her mother were at odds. Reflecting on her behavior now, Mila says she is very grateful to her mum for her custody. Many people she knew got hooked on drugs and did many stupid things. And her mum's guardianship helped her to avoid many problems.

Mila was young and beautiful. Her mother knew that if she worked only as a model, her daughter's career would be over in a few years. So Galina insisted that Mila star in the movies. So Jovovich got into the picture "Return to the Blue Lagoon". This film turned out to be beautiful, exciting, and of high quality. This is how popularity came to the girl.

Soon, she was involved in filming "Chaplin", where she played the main character's wife. Thus, already at the age of eighteen Mila became a star.

Then she married Sean Andrews. But, after a month, it became clear that young people are too hasty and took their passion and crush for a natural feeling. So they broke up, and Mila decided to do something new.

Mila has a beautiful voice. She recorded her album, which has one song in her native Ukrainian language. Her folk-inspired songs have always appealed to her fans. At one time, Jovovich toured the cities of the United States of America and European countries. And everywhere she was received "with flying colors".

But then Mila returned to filmmaking, and there was no more time for music. The reason for her return was to meet Luc Besson and star in the acclaimed, world-famous film The Fifth Element. At the Luc Besson casting for The Fifth Element, she appears without eyebrows (painted over them with glittery makeup) but on 20-centimeter platforms.

Besson calls the image vulgar and tasteless and refuses the role. But Mila is not too upset, as if she already knows that this encounter is not the last. In a few months, she notices the director at the hotel pool where she is staying and decides to go and say hello: "Hi, I'm the girl you didn't give a part to!" An alarmed Besson, who has been sunbathing peacefully, has no choice but to say give the part and fall in love.

"The Fifth Element brings Jovovich worldwide fame. The next picture of Besson with her participation, "Joan of Arc", ends with even greater success. Mila brilliantly pulled off the role. After this picture, the whole world talked about her. Jovovich woke up a trendy actress who wanted to see in their films many directors.

Mila married Luc Besson, then divorced him, but managed to star in several of his films. She is currently married to another director Paul Anderson. They have a daughter and are happily married.

Mila is proud that she is Ukrainian, knows the Ukrainian language, and goes to the Ukrainian church. So even though she lives in America, Jovovich always remembers where she comes from.

James Bond Girl Olga Kurylenko is also Ukrainian

The story of actress and model Olga Kurylenko is another Cinderella tale. A simple girl from the Ukrainian town of Berdyansk, she became a French citizen, 'Bond Girl' and Tom Cruise's partner in the film 'Oblivion'.

Today Olga Kurilenko calls herself a Frenchwoman of Ukrainian descent", although she arrived in France at quite an advanced age - at 16. She spent most of her childhood in Ukraine, in the city of Berdyansk. Olya had a large family, and everyone lived in the same flat, including her aunt, uncle, grandmother, grandfather, and cousin. But, as they usually say in such situations, "nothing foretold such a brilliant career".

Olga Kurylenko's parents ensured that she could achieve a lot in life. She studied English from 7 and attended music school and the ballet studio. In the future, knowledge of a foreign language will come in handy - after all, Kurylenko believes that the language barrier hampers most foreigners in Hollywood.

Unlike many stars who grew up in small towns, Olga likes not to talk about how she used to harvest potatoes or milk cows. She is very laconic in her recollections.

Biography of the family, which grew up and brought up the future actress, is hardly possible to call an exemplary and prosperous. Shortly after the birth of a daughter's father, Konstantin Kurilenko, left the family, and her mother had to raise Olya herself. Except for her and the little girl, the small flat was inhabited by Olga's aunt, uncle, and their son, who often stopped by and grandmother. So, when mum went to work, there was someone to look after the girl.

Olga Kurilenko grew up very active and curious: she adored India and admired everything connected with it; she spoke English and went to the drama studio and ballet. She did well at school, and her mother tried to encourage her. She knew that her daughter loved traveling more than anything else; traveling to different towns and villages was an incentive to get good grades.

Everything was just like in today's TV series: right in the Moscow metro, the young beauty was spotted by a representative of an international modeling agency. When he found out that the girl was just 13, he got distraught but still left her mother his contacts.

She did not take long to figure it out: she was saving a large part of her salary as a drawing teacher, and now she is keeping it "for Paris. Two years later, having amassed a modest portfolio, my daughter and mother came to Moscow to participate in a casting session. Three years passed, and this hobby, to which she devoted all her free time, got Olga to Paris. This seemed a pipe dream, but she managed to sign a contract with Madison's modeling agency to go to France and never return to her homeland - thus, Olga Kurylenko became 'a Frenchwoman of Ukrainian origin'.

Olga's career took off! Offers were pouring in one after the other, and the young star could hardly manage to receive them. Time was running out, but thanks to her hard work, the Ukrainian beauty found her way to the world's hottest glossy magazines in a matter of years: she shot up on the pages of Vogue, Madame Figaro, Elle, Marie Claire, and became the face of Lejaby lingerie. But Kurilenko wanted more - she believed she could be more than just a model; she wanted to be an actress.

How she longed for her homeland! At first, the most unpleasant thing about being in a foreign land was that she didn't speak French. To learn it properly - when? The language barrier caused various difficulties; because of this, Olya often cried, and more than once wanted to drop everything and return to Berdyansk. But her strong character and persistence got the upper hand after all. She decided to go ahead with whatever it might cost her.

In 1999, Olga's photos reached New York: they started to appear on giant billboards there. And she wondered whether the limits of modeling were too narrow. What if she tried her hand at the cinema? Prestigious courses helped her learn the basics of acting, and she enrolled without hesitation.

Determination and perseverance mean a lot - the newly minted actress soon was filming in full: first, there were episodic roles in various low-budget and not very popular films. But you have to start somewhere.

Olga got her first starring role in an erotic film, "The Call of Love," six years later. Another year later, the film "Paris, I Love You," came out on the screens, in which the partner was the famous Kurylenko "hobbit" Elijah Wood.

In 2007, Olga played the lead female role in "Hitman," the partner of her character Nicky Voronina was Timothy Olyphant. After that, she glorified the image of a femme fatale beauty capable of standing up for herself. She was recognized and loved.

In 2008, she received the proposal of her life. No, not marriage. She was chosen for the 'Bond Girl' role in the Bondiana series Quantum of Solace. It was then that the world recognized Olga.

By her admission, Kurylenko has not become a hostage to her role. In any case, she does not feel the 'Bond girl' stamp on her. This shooting has brought her popularity and a lot of valuable acquaintances for the further conquest of Hollywood. However, with Daniel Craig, who played Bond, she never became friends; somehow, it did not work out.

And although many will remember her as one of the heroines of the "Bondiana" or the star of the film "Oblivion" with Tom Cruise, Kurylenko herself believes that the primary victory is still ahead. The actress dreams of working with director Lars von Trier and even invites him to consider her candidacy.

About her personal life, Olga Kurilenko does not like to spread. "Don't think of me as secret," she explains, "but private is private. Especially when things are not so easy in one's personal life. I'm afraid to scare away my happiness or rush things.

Things weren't easy. Officially Olga has been married three times; she first decided to tie the knot at 20. Her chosen one was the French photographer Cédric van Mol. It was this union that helped the future star to obtain French citizenship. As is often the case, love lasted for three years, and the couple decided to divorce.

Olga married entrepreneur Damian Gabriel from the USA for the second time, but even this marriage was not strong. And finally, for the third time, Kurylenko went under the crown with a Mexican businessman, whose name remained a mystery. She did not go out in public with a mysterious lover, and soon, just as in an atmosphere of secrecy and without any fuss, they broke up.

The actress believes that men with her "very difficult. Moreover, by her admission, Olga never wanted to get married; the circumstances just happened: "I understand, it's pretty strange to hear it from a man who has been married three times, but I never wanted to get married. By the way, the second time I did it just for him, because he asked very, very, very much. After the first marriage, I said: "I won't do it again." But he said: "It's essential to me." What you don't do for the person you love! "

The star is now in a de facto marriage to British writer and journalist Max Benicio, with whom she gave birth to a son, Alexander Marc Horatio Benicio, on October 3, 2015, writes Clutch.ua.

Olga Kurylenko is a sought-after actress and model, a loving wife, and a happy mother. Her story once again proves that nothing is impossible in this world.

Interesting facts about Olga Kurylenko

In 2013, Olga Kurylenko was ranked 30th in Men's Health magazine's sexiest women, writes uznaivse.ru.

Olga speaks four languages fluently - Ukrainian, Russian, French, and Spanish.

In 2008 she won the prestigious Elle Style Awards in the 'Breakthrough of the Year' category.

For her role in the film "Quantum of Solace" in 2009 received the "Saturn" award in the category "Best Supporting Actress", as well as the UK Film Award "Empire" as "Best Actress".

Serge Lifar - "God of Dance", An Ardent Patriot of Kyiv, The Loyal Friend of Coco Chanel

Serge Lifar, the legendary French dancer and choreographer, was called the "God of Dance". Despite this, he always reminded everyone of his Ukrainian origins and never forgot his homeland.

Sergiy Lifar was born on April 15, 1905, in Kyiv, in the family of an official, Mikhail Yakovlevich Lifar and Sofia Vasilyevna Marchenko-Lifar. He studied at the Imperial Alexander Gymnasium in Kyiv, was fond of music, and had a true passion for dance. Since childhood, his big dream had been to learn how to dance ballet.

Throughout his life, Serge Lifar was also engaged in literary work: he wrote articles, kept diaries, corresponded a lot, and told about his life on the pages of his memoirs "Memories of Icarus". The artist's autobiography provides a unique opportunity to trace first-hand the tumultuous path of his life, with its ups and downs. It is a memoir of his youth in Kyiv, the city which Lifar adored all his life while in exile. It is an emotional and heartfelt confession about building an incredible career in Paris, a story about his development as an artist and a person.

In his autobiography, Lifar recalls the early 1920s in Kyiv and how frightened he was by the horror that came to his beloved city with the Soviets. He was once in the opera house in Kyiv to attend a class with the famous choreography teacher Bronislava Nizhinskaya. He admits that she was skeptical of his dancing abilities at first, but by some miraculous coincidence, he was one of the lucky five dancers who were sent to Monte Carlo to dance with the Russian Ballet Company at Sergei Diaghilev's request.

It was the beginning of a new phase in his life when a completely different world suddenly opened up before the sixteen-year-old boy. He discovered Europe with its possibilities and was able to return to Ukraine as late as 1961. Lifar never saw his mother again.

"Can you imagine what it meant for a young boy from wintry Ukraine - from abject poverty and daily fear to suddenly find himself in the fairytale world of Monaco, with the blue sea, clear skies, lush gardens, and omnipresent luxury on the show?" asks Serge Lifar in his memoirs.

Serge Diaghilev and Serge Lifar enjoyed a close friendship until he died in 1929. Diaghilev, who had an uncanny knack for talent, was quick to recognize the great potential in Lifar. He was convinced that he would make an incredible dancer, and he willingly undertook to train and develop Serge.

Describing his experience of becoming an artist, Lifar recalls with great respect: "Diaghilev decided to fulfill his greatest dream with me. He sought to develop all my abilities, to teach me everything. He opened art in all its forms before me, combining painting, music, and dance - through museums and churches in Italy, surprising me with his instinctive fine taste and exuberant temperament. He was a demanding teacher, almost a tyrant."

In 1929, at the age of 24, Serge Lifar took over the direction of the Paris Grand Opéra, not suspecting that he would remain there for almost thirty years. He became more than just a theatrical star, choreographer, soloist, and teacher for the French ballet. Serge Lifar revived the glory of French ballet, becoming its reformer and the founder of a new trend - classicism. "Icarus" is one of the most famous ballets of the time, which became a kind of personification of Lifar himself.

"Often in my nightmares, the style of my new work, my choreography, was born, and I woke up and wrote it down. How many times at night, in the abyss of the world, I looked at the civilizations of our planet, or perhaps other planets," wrote Serge Lifar.

The Second World War was a trying time for Serge Lifar. He witnessed the German occupation of Paris and made the firm decision not to leave the French capital. Despite the constant risks, threats, and harassment, Lifar stayed with the opera. He shoulders a huge responsibility - to ensure that French culture does not collapse.

He is also worried about Kyiv, where he is outraged by the destruction of the city center, trees, and old houses. Memories of cozy Kyiv, its history, and its views have always been present in the artist's thoughts. In 1941, when the Germans occupied the Ukrainian capital, Serge Lifar published an article entitled' Kyiv My Hometown' on the front page of the French edition Paris-Midi, which provoked a wave of anger among Paris's top occupation authorities.

In an article dubbed 'nationalist', Lifar wrote: "Kyiv, my hometown. I lived a happy and smiling childhood, then awkward adolescence, tormented by war and revolution, then a youth full of adventure. I left in 1922, when I was seventeen, for a new world - the world of dance. I took the love of my hometown with me. I love it; I will always love it with all my being. I will be an ardent patriot of Kyiv till my last breath".

Serge Lifar was friends with many iconic figures: Pablo Picasso, Erik Satie, Serge Prokofiev, Igor Stravinsky, and others. His friendship with Jean Cocteau and Coco Chanel was intense. Pablo Picasso produced many drawings by Serge Lifar, including portraits and sketches in ballet class.

"Picasso and Chanel became my godparents in the art world. Each passed on a piece of their secret to me. Chanel - the tireless search through layout and separation, the courage to take everything apart after months of work and return to its original and pure simplicity," Serge Lifar told me.

Like Coco Chanel, Lifar spent the last years of his life in Lausanne, Switzerland. He is buried in the Saint-Genevieve-des-Bois cemetery.

Legendary American Singer Kvitka Cysyk, with a Ukrainian Heart

Kvitka Cisyk was born on April 4, 1953, to a family of Ukrainian immigrants in upstate New York. Her voice was much admired in American showbiz. She has worked with Michael Jackson, Whitney Houston, and other international stars.

She was one of the most expensive and popular jingle performers in the US during her career. She could be seen and heard in Mcdonald's, American Airlines, Coca-Cola, and Ford Motor advertising campaigns.

The singer's full name is Kvitoslava. Her family and friends used to call her a flower. And she gained fame in the US under the artistic pseudo - Kacey - a combination of the first letters of her name and surname - Kvitka Cisyk.

Kvitka Cisyk's father was a violinist in Lviv. Her grandparents and mother lived in Lviv until 1944. The family was prominent intellectuals in the city. Fleeing the occupation and the Soviets, they found themselves in the United States in 1949. The singer was already born in New York in 1953. As a child, Kvitka was a scout - she traveled to camps in the mountains to learn Ukrainian songs, customs, and rituals.

Cisyk had a coloratura soprano voice. Her fans could sometimes guess the sound of a violin in her voice. She experimented with styles from jazz to classical with ease. And she has had great success with pop songs as well as opera singing. She also had a technique common to Carpathian villages - the 'white voice'.

After her father died, Kvitka was forced to seek additional sources of income: she offered recordings to various companies and sang in clubs in New York. That's how she got noticed by producers. Since then, Cisyk has become one of America's most famous and expensive jingle singers. Her voice has been heard in Coca-Cola, American Airlines, and McDonald's commercials. For 16 years and the rest of her life, she was the official voice of Ford Motors. Many Americans still remember the musical jingle "Have you driven A Ford lately" performed by Kasey Cisyk. Ford gave her cars for that. The same company estimated that Cisyk's voice has listened to more than 22 billion times, which is several times more than the world's population.

In 1978 the song You Will Light Up My Life, sung by Kvitka Cisyk in the film of the same name, won her an Oscar and a Golden Globe. The song was also nominated for a Grammy in Song of the Year. Cisyk sang all the female parts in the film, although her name was cut from the credits due to a conflict with the director. In the movie Kvitka Cisyk also tried herself as an actress, playing the role of a friend of the main character.

The singer worked and assisted many famous American musicians and producers. She sang backing vocals for Whitney Houston and Michael Jackson. She has also been invited by well-known singers such as Michael Bolton, Bob James,Linda Ronstadt, and Roberta Flack to participate in recording their albums.

In the Cisyk family, both daughters were musically gifted. Their parents taught Kvitka and her older sister Maria to play the violin and piano from a young age. Maria became a famous pianist and was director of the San Francisco Conservatory.

Kvitka Cisyk recorded two Ukrainian-language albums, "Flower" in 1980 and "Two Colours" in 1989. It cost her around $200,000. To record them, she hired the best musicians in New York; Kvitka was accompanied by her sister Maria, and her mother gave the correct Ukrainian pronunciation.

Both records were nominated for a Grammy Award in 1990 in the "contemporary folk" category. They were mostly smuggled into Ukraine, with people re-recording the songs and passing them on to each other.

Kvitka Cisyk has only been to Ukraine once. She came to Lviv in 1983 with her mother, but the trip was not publicized and was almost secret.

There was a ban on Cisyk in Soviet Ukraine as her repertoire included songs from the UPA and the Secession Streltsy. After Ukraine's independence, Tsisyk had planned to come to Ukraine for a concert; however, this plan was never realized.

Cisyk had two American husbands. Both were musicians, and both worked on her Ukrainian songs. Her son Ed-Vladimir is also involved in music.

In 1992 doctors informed Kvitka of the diagnosis of breast cancer. They measured a few months of her life, which lasted seven years. Kvitka died five days short of her 45th birthday. Her mother and sister died of the same disease.

Vladimir Horowitz - King of Pianists from Kiev

Vladimir Horowitz is a pianist who cannot be copied, a symbol of 20th century piano playing, the most unpredictable musician of our time, 25-time winner of several Grammy Awards, the highest award in the world of music.

The twentieth century can safely be called a century of great pianists: Paderewski, Hoffmann, Rachmaninoff, Richter, Rubinstein, Kempf. The list could go on endlessly. But above all of these geniuses, Vladimir Horowitz stands out for the average music lover and the professional historian.

He, and not anyone else, is rightly regarded as the symbol of twentieth-century pianism. He has become the consummate performer of modern classical music, presenting the works of Sergei Prokofiev to American audiences. Even his detractors agree with him. One may not like Horowitz, but one cannot deny that he is exceptional.

Much has been written about Horowitz. His performance style, which they called "Horowitzian", was considered by critics to be "too pretentious". He has been called "the most unpredictable musician of our time", "a genius of communication", "an electric charge of 6000 volts", and "the king of all pianists".

Vladimir Horowitz is presented in the World Music Encyclopaedia as an "American pianist", but the future virtuoso was born in Kyiv on October

1, 1903. In Ukraine, he was formed a personality and received a musical education. Articles and research, as a rule, focus on his life and work after 1925, that is, after his move to Western Europe. Very little is known about the Kyiv period. But the sources of the formation of the great pianist's craftsmanship are most interesting. After all, Horowitz represents one of the most potent performing schools in the history of pianism.

The first lessons Vladimir received were given to him by his mother. However, when Vladimir was 12 years old, everyone thought that he would grow up to be a composer but not a pianist who would change the world and remain at the top for almost 70 years. In 1912, when Horowitz was nine years old, he began studying at the Kyiv Conservatory with Sergei Tarnovsky and Felix Blumenfield. Although Horowitz was not known as a self-taught composer, no master could have given him the skill he had achieved. Horowitz discovered his unusual musical talent at the age of ten when he had memorized all of Wagner's works.

The revolution of 1917 did not do the Horowitz family any good. The house the family lived in was confiscated, as were their possessions. Within a day, almost everything was taken - even their clothes. But that was not what struck the 14-year-old boy the most. It was the incomprehensible fact that "the Bolsheviks stole my piano". This resentment probably motivated his decision not to return to the USSR in 1926.

But he continued to study at the Conservatoire, giving concerts to earn money to support himself and his family. Two years later, Horowitz graduated from the Conservatoire, where he graduated with a performance of Rachmaninoff's Third Piano Concerto - an extraordinarily complex but at the same time exciting work with which he was yet to meet a fate more than once.

Horowitz's first audiences were the people of Kyiv, Kharkiv, and Odesa. He then enjoyed fantastic success in Moscow and Leningrad. Together with the violinist Nathan Milstein, Horowitz toured cities in Ukraine and Russia. He gave three concerts a day and, until 1925, had twelve concert programs in his repertoire (usually, a professional pianist would have one or two). In Leningrad, for example, in 1924, Vladimir gave 11 concerts in two months, in which he performed 155 pieces!

When Vladimir left Kyiv for good, he was already an established pianist and had a brilliant career abroad. Horowitz's first concert outside the Soviet Union took place in Berlin in 1926. He gave 69 shows on a European tour in one year and was enormously acclaimed.

For almost three years, Vladimir toured practically all of Europe with concerts, enjoying tremendous success. In Paris, when he played, the gendarmes were even summoned to silence the audience, who were smashing chairs in Catharsis.

Quite amusingly, his career started in Europe. The work that made him known to the general public was Tchaikovsky's famous First Concerto. It happened like this: in a hotel in Germany, a pretty unknown performer was approached and offered to replace a female soloist who suddenly felt ill. "Can you play in two hours?" - Vladimir was asked. He agreed.

Without a single rehearsal, the pianist went out into the hall. The conductor was the already venerable musician Eugene Pabst. They talked a bit about the tempo of the performance, and the conductor, not hoping for a successful evening anymore, simply asked the pianist to follow the orchestra. The success was frantic. The stunned audience gave him a standing ovation.

In 1933 Horowitz married Wanda Toscanini, the daughter of the world-famous conductor.

Since then, the musician has been welcomed into the circle of the American aristocracy. He commissioned a unique grand piano; his private art collection included paintings by Picasso and Degas and many other things that only a few could afford. He had everything except those he loved.

His mother died shortly after he left the Soviet Union, and his father was sent to the Gulag as the father of an 'enemy of the people. His beloved sister Regina modestly taught music at the Kharkiv Conservatoire for the rest of her life, though Vladimir recalled that she was an even better pianist than he was. Sad news from his homeland, and the feeling that the superficial American public was incapable of understanding the intrinsic value of the music he played, caused Vladimir to become depressed.

After the 1953 anniversary, Horowitz stopped his concert activities for 12 years and made only a few recordings. And his triumphant return took place on the Carnegie Hall stage in 1965. A crowd of fans lined up for tickets sold out in two hours!

The musician has performed twice at the White House for Presidents Herbert Hoover (1931) and Ronald Reagan (1989), receiving the American Medal of Freedom award from the latter.

During his years in the USA, Horowitz has won 25 Grammy awards (the same number as Stevie Wonder) in various categories - the fifth-highest number in Grammy Awards history.

The documentary film The Last Romantic (1985) was made about the life of Horowitz, and the musicologist David Dubal has published a book, Evenings with Horowitz.

Maria Primachenko is a Unique Ukrainian Artist of International Renown

As we see Maria Primachenko in most of the pictures, this simple village woman does not look like a "star" of naive art, an honored artist, People's Artist of Ukraine, in whose honor the small planet 14624 was named. She received the elite title during her lifetime - justly and deservedly for her incredible, fairytale-like vision of the world. At the same time, she did not live as "deserved" - all 88 years of her life in her native village Bolotnya in the Kyiv region, without special favors or conditions.

UNESCO devoted a whole year to her - 2009, art critics and biographers have conducted research, and encyclopedias and Wikipedia have written voluminous articles.

During her lifetime, the artist sometimes referred to herself as Pryj-machenko, explaining that Primachenko was a Russified version of herself. The paintings were signed only by Primachenko or M. P. P. The correctness of the spelling of the surname became acute after the artist's death - after the presidential decree on the celebration of the 100th anniversary of the birth of Maria Primachenko - with the letter "i".

Maria's mother, Praskovia Vasilyevna, was a master embroiderer. Probably, she passed on to the artist a sense of form and color, as well as the ability to beautifully embroider - all her shirts Maria embroidered for herself until her old age. Her father, Aksentiy Grigorievich, was also gifted in art: he was a carpenter, but the yard fences he made with his own hands were made in the form of head pictures.

As a child, Primachenko contracted polio. At the time, childhood mortality from the disease reached 90 percent. Maria survived. The disease taught her to concentrate well but also made her very vulnerable.

Unexpected fame came to Primachenko at the age of 27. In 1936, the "communist government" wanted to see the people in the arts and attracted rural nuggets to study. Maria was invited to Kyiv to learn in experimental workshops at the Kyiv Museum of Ukrainian Art. She was so fond of her works that they were exhibited at the first Republican Exhibition of Folk Art the same year, and a separate hall was allocated for them.

She then traveled to exhibitions in Moscow, Leningrad, Warsaw, Paris, Sofia, Montreal, and Prague. Finally, in her homeland, she was awarded a diploma and a gold medal at an international exhibition in Paris. At a distance, of course. Maria was in her native village at the time.

She met her husband (as it turned out, her countryman) at Kievo-Pecherskaya Lavra. She was 27 and studying at the School of National Masters, situated in the monastery's territory. And Vasiliy Marinchuk, lieutenant of the Red Army, had just arrived for the excursion. It turned out that the boy was from a neighboring village. The young men fell in love with each other.

Barely finishing her studies, Maria left Kyiv, though she could have stayed here, and went to the village to her beloved.

The artist has never been officially married. With her husband, Vasily Marinchuk lived almost five years in a civil marriage. In 1941 Maria gave birth to a son, Fyodor, just as the Second World War began. The man mobilized and did not return from the war.

Another of Primachenko's talents was wedding dough. The artist not only painted masterpieces and deftly embroidered, she also baked various items for weddings and was famous for these in her village.

The artist was right-handed but painted with her left hand. She did not know any professional tricks. She had no art education and painted with simple gouache and watercolor on a standard piece of cotton paper.

Despite her fairytale-like, fantastical, naïve imagery, the artist did not skimp on pressing issues. In 1936 she painted 'Animal Trial'. On it, a black monkey at the table is writing the record, and two wolves are standing in front of it on tiptoe - not difficult to guess that this is an association with the communist repressions. In one of her paintings from the 1930s, she depicted an elephant-like monster and captioned it: "The beast walks and searches for food, no outfit on its mind when it wants to eat" - a reference to the Holodomor, perhaps?

In 1986 Maria created a series dedicated to Chornobyl because her native village Bolotnya is located almost 30 km away from the Chornobyl nuclear power plant.

A highlight of Primachenko's paintings is captions and jokes. She wrote and rhymed them herself or adapted folk sayings to the subject of her painting. "The three Busliks in the peas live with us to this day", "Lejeune lay down under the apple tree so that the apple itself fell into his mouth, and it fell into his forehead", "Galya fed the pigs on the farm. She raised a thousand and seventy piglets", "The hens are dancing and plowing bread", "Ada the doggy is not afraid of gad", "Freckles-horns - cheerful birds" - all captions strike with childishness and depth at the same time.

The artist has illustrated books and collaborated with Ukrainian writer Mikhail Stelmakh. Primachenko created drawings for the Ukrainian writer's books The Crane and The Stork Takes a Shower. She also illustrated five children's books for the publishing house "Raduga". And it was children's drawings that she invented, rather than adapting or giving her ready-made pictures.

Prymachenko borrowed the style from the famous Marimekko brand and was accused of plagiarism. The plagiarism came to light six years after Marimekko applied the 'forest people' picture from its designer Cristina Izola to its home products and textiles. The same image was put on the planes of FinnAir Airlines, which cooperated with Marimekko. And everything would be fine if not for the strange resemblance of "forest people" to the Ukrainian artist's "rat on the road". The only difference in the paintings was no rat in the Finnish designer's subject. When a scandal erupted thanks to a journalist's observation, Marimekko and Ms. Isola acknowledged plagiarism and apologized for the incident, while FinnAir removed the drawings from their aircraft. In Finland, however, Ukrainian artist Maria Primachenko will always be remembered.

Summary

U kraine is a country in the center of Europe with an ancient history and tradition. Its unique culture combines the best practices of Western civilization and Eastern Slavicism. Ukraine has come a long way since gaining its independence, but its people have not submitted, and in our time, they continue to fight bravely for their freedom.

In our book, we have covered only a few pages and told about exciting traditions of Ukrainians, their cuisine, a celebration of holidays, famous people of the past and present, and famous monuments and sights of the country. There is, in fact, so much to tell about this fascinating country that if you want to learn more about it, you should visit it for yourself.

Made in the USA
Middletown, DE
12 November 2024

64424653R00075